2⁴⁰

PROBLEMS
and
PROGRESS

A Theological and
Psychological Inquiry

Edited by ROBERT W. GLEASON, S.J.

Learning and religion are liberating forces, especially to be prized in an era of doubt and confusion such as ours. Fully convinced of the peculiar needs of today and the relevance of learning and religion for their solution, nine authors have undertaken to examine specific areas with which they have been especially concerned.

These essays were originally read as papers during a lecture series in the School of General Studies of Fordham University, under the direction of Rev. Charles O'Neill, S.J., Dean of the School of General Studies. It is the fervent hope of all the authors that this volume may make some small contribution to the needs of the age and the advancement of reason and faith.

Problems and Progress

PROBLEMS

and

PROGRESS

A Theological and Psychological Inquiry

EDITED BY ROBERT W. GLEASON, S.J.

The Newman Press · 1962 · Westminster, Maryland

Nihil obstat: EDWARD A. CERNY, S.S., S. T.D.
           Censor librorum

Imprimatur: ✠ LAWRENCE J. SHEHAN, D.D.
           Archbishop of Baltimore
           May 22, 1962

The *nihil obstat* and *imprimatur* are official declarations that a book or pamphlet is free of moral and doctrinal error. No implication is contained therein that those who have granted the *nihil obstat* and *imprimatur* agree with the opinions expressed.

Table of Contents

Foreword

THE PRESENT VOLUME mirrors in a way the complexity of the modern Christian world. It presents a very varied series of essays on crucial questions which center on perennial themes of man in his relationship to God and other men.

The peculiar psychological tensions of our age with its complex and even unique theological preoccupations have created special needs and urgent problems. No simple solution exists, and in fact no single solution is possible. Nevertheless, the light of reason and faith is powerful enough to dissipate many obscurities if allowed to shine unimpeded. Learning and religion are liberating forces, especially to be prized in an era of doubt and confusion such as ours. Fully convinced of the peculiar needs of today and the relevance of learning and religion for their solution, nine authors have undertaken to examine specific problems with which they have been especially concerned. The changes brought about in the city parish by the rapid shifts of population and the problem created by mass immigration are discussed by Rev. Joseph Fitzpatrick, S.J., in his sociological analysis of the city parish. The theological implications of the vast "image industries" and the Church's effort to meet these new challenges are outlined by Monsignor Flynn. In his paper on evolution and Catholic theology, Rev. J. Franklin Ewing, S.J., puts in proper perspective the much-discussed themes of biological evolution and its relationship to the Catholic Faith; in the process he cleans the ground of a number of widely accepted myths. Rev. William Hurley, S.J., outlines the disintegrating forces implicit in discriminatory attitudes not only from the point of view of society but also from the viewpoint of the individual Christian.

Emilio Dido confronts Freudian psychology with the positions of St. Thomas Aquinas and points up the difference of perspective of each as well as the fundamental contributions of Sigmund Freud to a deeper understanding of man's psychology. In his essay on mental health and Catholicism, Rev. George Hagmaier applies many of the insights of psychoanalytical theory to the Christian life and shows how they can be integrated into a fuller Christian life. Rev. Robert W. Gleason, S.J., reviews the contribution of a number of contemporary philosophers to the understanding of the nature and function of marital love. The delicate relationships of the Catholic in the field of Church-State are explored by Rev. Joseph Costanzo, S.J., who clarifies many of the problems that beset the Catholic in a pluralistic society. Rev. John Lafarge, S.J., in his "Hallmark of Dedication" sounds a clear call to responsible Christian living, involving commitment to the Catholic issues of the day.

The essays in the present volume were originally read as papers during a lecture series in the School of General Studies of Fordham University, under the direction of Rev. Charles O'Neill, S.J., Dean of the School of General Studies. When their appearance in book form was suggested by The Newman Press, each author revised his work for publication.

It is the fervent hope of all the authors that this little volume may make some small contribution to the needs of the age and the advancement of reason and faith.

Problems and Progress

Hallmarks of Dedication

REV. JOHN LaFARGE, S.J.*

CONTEMPORARY MAN cannot escape the problem of images. The recent election campaign was a war of images. We can no longer plead ignorance of world conditions since we have ample means on every side to acquaint ourselves with them. Nor can we plead ignorance of the world's misery and suffering. Each of us is confronted with a moral issue—the choice between acting responsibly or irresponsibly. Responsibility is a favorite word in our time; in fact, it is a modern phenomenon to use "responsibility" in an absolute sense; without indicating responsibility to what or to whom. But from its nature the word implies an answer, an interrogator. Today we leave that problem in the air and simply ask for responsibility. The president's re-

* For more than fifty years a Jesuit priest, Father LaFarge has been on the staff of *America* since 1926. He was its editor-in-chief from 1944 to 1948. His own widely read autobiography, *The Manner is Ordinary,* has been translated into French and enjoys an American paperback edition. He founded the first Catholic Interracial Council in New York in 1934.

port demands responsible action on the part of American citizens, constructive action of which we can give an account. When that question is raised, one thinks of the alternatives. We can evade the issue, as many do, simply putting it out of their minds. If there is a program on television—a documentary which stresses some of these problems—it is an easy thing to flip over to another channel.

For most of us here in the United States, the issue of human distress, human poverty, is more or less academic. The present generation is growing up without direct experience of poverty or persecution, homelessness and terror. To talk about sad things merely creates boredom. How many young people have had the experience of hopeless poverty? Of the difficulty of getting meat to eat more than once a week? Of dealing with aged and helpless parents? Of facing starvation—absolute homelessness? Millions of people in this world are faced with these problems. Yet America's daily press or weekly press simply cannot continue to feature human misery. This is not the way to run a paper or create an interesting magazine. One features rather things that happen. But what about things that do not happen? One cannot run a headline stating that people of such a province are still in the same deplorable condition they have been in for the last three years. There is no news value in that. Yet that is reality. Let us take, for instance, the situation of the Arab refugees from Israel in the Gaza Strip about which there is widespread argument: still there, after more than ten years. Consider the deadlock between Israel and the United

Arab Republic. What can be done about it? People have lost interest in it. It is an old story; there is nothing new to say about it.

Father Benjamin Masse of the *America* staff recently returned from a trip around the world with a group of people in the company of Bishop Swanstrom, studying the relief work of the Church. All members of the laity, he agreed, were broken-hearted at what they saw in many places, as well as deeply moved by what the Church is doing against these terrible odds.

Television recently presented a brilliant showing of the new capitol of Brazil, Brasilia—a model capitol, a dream of modern functional architecture, the genius of Le Corbusier and Mies van der Rohe. Yet that same picture indicated that on the edge of the new city there remains the grim misery of a shoddy town, tin-can hovels and acute starvation.

Consider our own American Indians. Few of us know anything about the acute distress many of them experienced on our reservations. Our Plains Indians— we still have memories of their gallant days of adventure. But one does not feature their present condition in Westerns. No one would go to see the film. One can always forget those things or simply assume a pious attitude and say the Lord will take care of them: like the two pious men who went down the road to Jericho, saw the man in distress, commended him to the Lord, but did nothing about it. Perhaps because of our scant experience of physical and economic misery, we have little concept of the moral sufferings which accompany it. Again, a humanistic liberalism can take the form of enthusiastic sympathy for every and any good cause without thought of the damage mere enthusiasm may do to human liberty and basic human values. Liberalism may turn, as it did a few generations ago, to Communism or near-Communism and the remedy is worse than the disease.

Another way of evading the issue is to take refuge in various impractical schemes masked under the respectable name of conservatism or states' rights. If by states' rights is meant the states' responsibilities, well and good; but not so good if this means the refusal to bear a common burden as members of the nation. Kindred to this refusal is the unlimited defense of property rights which is sometimes propounded under the guise of rugged individualism. The property owner, in such a *laissez-faire* philosophy, has the absolute right to do anything he wants with his property, regardless of society. Then too, necessary vigilance against the infiltrations of Communism can degenerate into a crusade in which anti-Communism becomes an end in itself, based not on a serious analysis of the situation but on slogans, appeals to the emotions and suspicion. In this country we swing easily from one extreme to the other, from extreme left to extreme right. Sometimes we confuse the two as in the former Populist Movement in the Middle West. Such movements exert a strong attraction. They offer to people who otherwise feel insignificant a definite sense of power, power over one's fellow man, over the great and intangible forces that control the current world, over what is conceived as the dominant "establishment."

It would not be worthwhile to spend time on these aberrations were it not for the attraction they exert for certain types of Catholic collegians. They are infinitely more "fun" than the slow and the troublesome alternative. It is fun to run other people down as revenge for what your own people have suffered in the past. The children of recent immigrants have been some of the most intolerant people we have had in this country. No race or nation is immune to this temptation. It can take root anywhere. It can take root in Negro Africa. It is this vacuum in positive conviction, rather than the designs of Mr. Khrushchev, which constitutes the greatest peril for the United States.

In this connection, I would like to quote a statement by Lewis Webster Jones, Executive Secretary of the National Conference of Christians and Jews, who I think is a very wise and a moderate man:

Nihilism, the belief in nothing, is perhaps as great a danger as the Communist movement in America. Because, among other things, it gives Communism its greatest opportunity. People suffering from a pathological vacuum in belief may fall easy prey to the pathological leadership of a Hitler or a Stalin. Nihilism is something which cannot be investigated or rooted out by any committee on un-American activities. Nor is it completely at variance with the American tradition expressed in the Declaration of Independence and the Constitution. Nor can it be overcome or corrected by invocation of the familiar words of these great historical documents. I shall not attempt to catalogue all the sociological reasons pervading the American mood. Among these are big government, big industry, large-scale agriculture dependent on international markets and huge metropolitan complexes, enormous enrollments in schools, universities. All these things contribute to the erosion of a sense of individual responsibility. Few people feel that their personal actions can influence events. Having no power, they feel no responsibility.

That is a very pregnant sentence: "Having no power, people feel no responsibility." They tend to concentrate on their private lives and on "getting by." Lacking any guiding public philosophy, they conform to, rather than challenge, existing patterns of behavior. Irresponsibility, "don't care-ism" is not a healthy or stable mood. It is a spiritual affliction by no means confined to America. It is something which must be cured if we are to face the future with new confidence and to provide a solid backing for effective national leadership. Hence, we turn now to the other side of the picture, which is that of effective action, constructive action.

Let us make one point clear. It is not a question as to whether such constructive action *will be* taken. The Church, impelled and guided by the Spirit of truth, raises up men and women who will accomplish it. The Church's work is infinitely varied in the perpetual combat against human degradation. No individual person fully grasps this. Consider only what crosses my editorial desk every day—example is set, for instance, by the Young Christian Workers. One reads of a group of Young Christian Workers in Latin America, perhaps in Argentina. Here are a group of young people all of whom are desperately poor. Yet they manage to save from despair one of their colleagues by advising him, counselling him, helping him over his difficulty. This same type of effort takes place all over the world. African women wrestle with female slavery and the complicated plague of the bridal dowries—intelligent, thoughtful women struggling against centuries-old tribal tyranny. Consider the Opus Dei units of Catholic laymen who work in government offices; the charitable activities of our parishes, the various sodalities, the Third Order of St. Francis, our Catholic Interracial Councils—forty-five of them in this country working quietly and steadily to combat race prejudice. These are examples of the work which is going on. Most of us do not know what it is to face up to these problems. Once one has faced up to them, experienced them, how different is one's viewpoint! Again the Church's work is expressed by those whose philosophy is one of a poverty of means, without elaborate organization: the Little Brothers and Little Sisters of Charles de Foucauld who do their fraternal work among the poorest of the poor. Then too, how many dedicated young men and women go out to aid in the foreign missions.

The work of the Church is often done in an entirely different field—the intellectual field, the field of studies, of research. The work of the Church is advancing the intellectual frontiers of the kingdom of God. Not nearly as much of this work is done as might be, but still it counts. The real power of the Church is the power of the spirit. In the age-old history of Christianity, over and over again, from the days of Constantine, good people have tried to gain some other, more tangible form of power. It is all right, they feel, for the Church to bless kings and queens. It is quite right for the Church to work for just laws. It is right for the Church even to bless arms, guns and cannons to be used in self-defense. It is right for the Church to bless certain forms of force if they are used legitimately but this is not the *force of the Church*. The force of the Mystical Body is that of the Holy Spirit, of humility, of love, patience, suffering. It is the Church's only real power. All else can be esteemed and judged solely in the light of that supreme power—all her culture, her discipline. Consider for a moment our magnificent museums. These museums and art galleries are filled with the prodigal work of Christian artists and sculptors. Yet these objects too are significant only in the light of the Church's inner power. Otherwise, as St. Paul says, "they are but sounding brass and tinkling cymbal."

The question is not "What is there for me to do?" but "Do I let the work of the Church pass me by? Will my contribution be lost? Will I have lost the opportunity to build up my section of a new Jerusalem?"

The opposite of irresponsibility can be summed up in the word "dedication." Dedication is a question of free commitment and of the grace of God, of one serious decision, a major decision, followed later by an infinite number of micro-decisions springing from the original choice. The very word "dedication" opens up an infinite prospect. There are, however, certain "hallmarks" that such a decision should show. A hallmark was originally called such because in England gold and silver articles bore the marks of Goldsmith's Hall, that is, of official approval. Our action needs hallmarks. If action is to meet effectively the situation of the modern world it must fulfill certain basic conditions. These are the requirements for that genuine dedication or engagement for which the American bishops called in their recent statement. The bishops state that if our future is to be worthy of the past, if the future of America's promise is not to wither before it has reached full maturity, our present and pre-eminent need is to reaffirm the sense of individual obligation, to place clearly before ourselves the foundation upon which responsibility rests, to determine the causes of decay and the means by which the spirit of responsibility can be revived. The bishops have made a clear call to the laity of this country to exercise that individual initiative and total apostolic dedication which express the mission of the Church in the modern world. They require of each Catholic "a personal engagement" with the social and political communities that surround him as the result of a free and justified choice of careful reflection upon himself, his destiny, and the world.

As Catholics we cannot ignore the civic community around us. Our dedication, too, must be inspired by hope, not by cynicism or despair. Hope is not optimism —a feeling that things will somehow turn out all right. It is, rather, based on certainty and certainty is derived from the promises of God and rests upon revealed truth. Our greatest danger today is that lack of hope which is another form of the nihilism to which Dr. Jones referred. Hope is a trust inspired not by a foolish optimism but by a rock-bottom faith in the promises of God, in the eternal fidelity that He has manifested through the ages and has revealed in His Son. This implies hope not only in God, but in our fellow man, in his natural worth—disfigured though it be by original sin —and in his capacities.

Today there is a great deal of anxiety about the situation in the Congo. There is ample reason for anxiety. Yet what an error, both spiritual and practical, to take a completely pessimistic view of this situation. Granted that every people has certain natural powers, whatever their culture, we may always expect surprising results when we encourage them to develop those powers. He who considers a child merely a problem will never educate that child. If we look upon a child simply as a conundrum, as an enigma to be solved, we never succeed with him. If we look upon a child as a possibility, a hope to be realized, then we have the beginning of a policy. It is the same way with our neighbors. If we look upon them simply as a conundrum, something to be solved, we will never establish genuine relations with them. If we look upon the world simply as a problem to be solved, we will never develop a national policy. Our policy in dealing with other people, whether they are the old and cultivated people of Europe, the French or the Germans or the Spanish or the Africans, the people of Asia or our neighbors in America, must be based on an intense conviction that there are elements of good in them. These people have certain values, insights, potentialities. Our task is to be able to draw these out even though they may contradict us on many points. This is not foolish idealism, but human realism, realism in human relations. We must believe in our fellow man's natural worth, disfigured though it be by original sin; a belief nobly expressed in President Kennedy's report, which says of the Declaration of Independence—"that men were created equal and so on . . . was a mighty vision. That soaring vision enabled our society to meet the trials of emerging nationhood. It placed the young republic securely behind the principle that every human being is of infinite worth. In time it led the nation out of the morass of human slavery. It inspires us still in the struggle against injustice."

Our first condition is then that of hope; our second condition or hallmark is cooperation with others, sometimes in a close and complex organization, sometimes with individuals. If no visible person is nearby we can always work with the unseen members of the Mystical Body of Christ. The Church is always with us, laboring at our side. Even if one is a contemplative nun or a contemplative monk enclosed in a monastery, he or she is still working with the Church. One's engagement to constructive action means an engagement to live and work with others with all that this implies of patience, sincerity and truth. That of course implies a unity of purpose, a spirit of unity. We build that unity not by mere negative safeguards, but by a strong, an intense belief in the fundamental unity of the human race itself, its aims, hopes and desires. Unless we have that sense of unity which springs from the Christian vision, we will never be able to win the competition with the Communists in the world forum. What presents itself to underprivileged people, what impresses them, is the *unity* of the Communist scheme. Communist unity is not true unity; it is not a natural unity. It is unity based upon an idolatry of the material combined with an incredible marshalling of political tyranny. Nevertheless,

that forced unity is impressive and its cause is drama-
tized in vital and imaginative forms. True unity cannot
be manufactured. It must come from our inner conviction and our personal dedication as Catholics. It is our
task to arouse that spirit of unity among all our fellow
citizens; to be, as it were, the apostles both of charity
and of unity.

This leads us to the third hallmark of apostolic
dedication which is a positive commitment to the civic
world. Those words may sound a little dry, but every
now and then something happens to awaken us to
their meaning. Recently three firemen were killed in
the line of duty. Three young men, fathers of families.
Two of those men were struggling in a loft building to
disengage themselves from a heap of boxes that had been
piled up in defiance of the municipal fire laws. The
third man lost his life trying to extricate them. In five
years, in New York City, 61 firemen have died in the
line of duty and 12,632 have been injured. We may
think of their wives, of their children, of the shame to
the city of New York. Who is responsible? Are we to
say that such affairs do not concern us? Is our only concern to save our *own* soul? Such situations are my
responsibility. The precise responsibility depends upon
each person's circumstances. What is needed most is
commitment, dedication to the cause of God, the cause
of the Church. We must educate ourselves that we may
be better citizens. We must make our voices heard for
what is right by just and carefully reasoned protests.

All this adds up to the Way of the Cross. Our
constructive action springs from divine faith. I bear in

mind those for whom Christ died: all men. And I bear in mind for what He died: our resurrection to eternal glory, the kingdom of heaven. The only way to reconcile men with their differences and divisions is the Cross. I read the other day of an heroic Dutch missionary who worked in Borneo, where they have the delightful custom of hunting heads. Every young man is supposed to bring home, as trophy, a shrunken head. If he does, he is a hero. If he hesitates, he is a coward, despised. Girls taunt him. Prestige here is certified by a shrunken head. Does our prestige consist in shrinking the head of our enemy? It should consist in a very different triumph: shrinking our own pride and indifference. Each of us in our own fashion is called to be a follower of the Cross.

The Divided Allegiance of the Catholic

REV. JOSEPH F. COSTANZO, S.J.*

IT IS AN unpleasant experience in American politics that the Catholic Faith of an American citizen becomes a stirring issue almost solely when he runs for the highest magistracy of the land, the office of the president of the United States. The national debates of 1924, 1928, and 1960 have made this incontestably clear. There seems to be no insurmountable problem about any other office of public trust, military or civil, federal, state, or foreign service, legislative, judicial, executive. But let an American Catholic aspire to the presidency and the air is filled with refined insinuations and raucous warnings. At its worst, anti-Catholicism is a witches' brew of blinding bias, inherited prejudices, and stubborn prepossessions. On a much higher plane,

* Father Costanzo is assistant professor of political philosophy at Fordham University and is a member of the *Woodrow Wilson Foundation Awards Committee.* He lectured in Europe as an American specialist during the Summer of 1960 at the invitation of the Department of State. He was the author of many articles in American and European publications.

it seems possible to disengage anti-Catholicism from crude forms of bigotry and from the clutter of irrational motivations which inspired and characterized the Nativist and Know Nothing movements of the pre-Civil War period, from the American Protective Association movement after the Civil War and the repellent vulgarities of the Ku Klux Klan after World War I. Many non-Catholics of deep piety and great learning who are respectful friends of the Catholic Church have unresolved doubts and anxieties about a Catholic in the White House. We owe it to them in charity to explain ourselves just as we ought to acknowledge that they are honest in their criticisms and fears.

Anti-Catholicism in its rational core is a composite of three apprehensions: a Catholic, it is said, by reason of his spiritual allegiance to the papacy, as his Faith prescribes, is subject to the foreign jurisdiction of the pope, who is also a temporal sovereign. This obedience to the papacy in faith and morals, it is alleged, can and may operate in conflict with the American citizen's oath to uphold and obey the laws of his country. Secondly, the religious dogmatism of Catholicism is dialectically incompatible with political democracy. Doctrinal dogmatism and intolerance conduce to political dogmatism, civil intolerance, and absolutism, while, on the contrary, religious and philosophical relativism promotes civil tolerance and political democracy. Thirdly, the growth of Catholicism poses a grave threat to the existence of Protestantism. A numerically superior Catholic electorate might be tempted to change the Constitution in order to restrict the exercise of religious freedom for non-Catholics.

None of these suppositions is flimsy, nor will a satisfactory explanation dispel all lingering doubts and suspicions. The Catholic and non-Catholic worlds (and they are distinct worlds) have too long been divided by diverse histories which have engendered adverse habits of biased appraisals of one another.

First, then, let us consider the divided allegiance of the Catholic. In its most acute form this is a relatively modern problem that arose with the emergence of the national secular state and deepened with the Reformation. Historically, the early Christians were the first to protest against the overweening pretensions of a pagan omnicompetent state, that "we ought to obey God rather than men," without denying Caesar's due. For centuries thereafter, long before legal positivism hammered its shattering blows, all men held fast to the universal supremacy of the moral law, to the primacy of the spiritual over the temporal, to the moral and practical necessity of a plurality of allegiances complementary to one another. No one questioned the moral-legal continuum.

In the fifth century Pope Gelasius distinguished the separate spheres of jurisdiction for the spiritual and temporal empowerments. Both authorities are from God, each superior to and independent of the other in the legitimate exercise of power over the proper objects of its competence. Unfortunately, a turbulent history, the unsettling of legal and political institutions by the bar-

barian invasions, and the blending of the two powers in the same hands, now secular, now ecclesiastic, did not provide the tranquil conditions for the evolution of Church-State relations envisioned by the Gelasian formula. The enormous religious and political problems that followed upon the breakup of the unity of medieval Christendom were complicated almost beyond hope by the generally prevailing consensus on all sides that political allegiance depended upon and demanded religious uniformity. The Peace of Westphalia in 1648 simply froze the question without solving it by the expedient arrangement of *cuius regio eius religio.*

Our American colonists were heirs of these religious-political tensions. Many of them came to the new world to escape religious persecution and civil disabilities inflicted by the State-Church establishments of the old world and then, with a remarkable loss of memory, proceeded to set up their own Church establishments, often with intolerable restrictions for dissenters in their midst.

The fear of foreign domination through an ecclesiastical agency was widely evident during most of the colonial period and became increasingly acute as the movement for political independence gained momentum. It was in no way exclusively or even mainly an anti-Catholic bias. Seven of the ten established churches were of the Church of England. For a complex of reasons these were without bishops during the entire colonial period despite the genuine need for their spiritual ministrations. It was feared that English bishops, being sworn supporters of the crown and members of the House of Lords, would be unlikely to support the colonies in political issues. Besides, the defection of a number of their leaders who sympathized with the British government to loyal British colonies in Nova Scotia and other parts of Canada did not endear them to the rank and file of the people as the revolutionary cause became more clearly defined. There was too much opposition from those disaffected with the course of the Reformation in the Church of England. Presbyterians, Congregationalists, and Baptists viewed with alarm the prospects of an Anglican prelacy in their midst with all its historic ties with the crown and reminiscent of the persecutions they had fled from in the homeland. It is within the context of this all-pervading opposition to the presence of a foreign prelacy in the colonies that we must view the Laity Remonstrance of 1765 in which two hundred and fifty Catholic laymen of Maryland protested against the appointment of the Bishop of Quebec as their apostolic vicar. Charles Carroll of Annapolis, father of Charles Carroll of Carrolton, wrote at the time to Bishop Challoner:

Your Lordship must know, yet for many years past attempts have been made to establish a Protestant bishop on this continent, and yet such attempts have been as constantly opposed through the fixed aversion the people of America in general have to a person of such character. If such is the aversion of Protestants to a Protestant bishop, with what an eye will they look upon an Apostolic Vicar?

In 1784 the Maryland clergy addressed a memorial to Pope Pius VI in which they advised against the designation of a bishop, reporting that a superior *in spiritualibus* would suffice for the spiritual needs of the faithful. Father John Carroll, in a letter to Cardinal Antonelli (dated February 27, 1785), perhaps gave the most acute expression to the colonial aversion to a foreign bishop when he urged that Rome permit the Catholic clergy to select their own native ecclesiastical superior. He called attention to the sixth of the Articles of Confederation that "no one who holds office under the United States shall be allowed to receive any gift, office or title of any kind whatsoever from any king, prince or foreign government."

Carroll was of the opinion that this prohibition extended only to those appointed to public office in the republic but added significantly "it will perhaps be wrested by our opponents to apply also to ecclesiastical offices."

Though the construction which was rightly placed upon the Anglican bishop's tie to the British Crown should not have applied to the Catholics' religious allegiance to the papacy, nevertheless the Catholic colonials were eager not to give any grounds to this misconception. With political independence, the Protestant Episcopalian Church in the United States was freed from its oath of fealty to the Crown and gradually became entirely self-governing in its ecclesiastical jurisdiction, though it continued in regular communion with all branches of the Anglican Church. While Catholics on their part developed a native American hierarchy, the fear of popery continued to linger in American minds and at different times and for varying reasons would come to the surface and even erupt into open violence. Such occasions were the rising rate of Catholic immigration, disputes about Bible reading and sectarian religious indoctrination in public schools, episcopal requests for tax support of Catholic parochial schools, and legislation about divorce, birth control, and sterilization.

What shall we say about the implications of foreign jurisdiction in the Catholics' allegiance to the pope, who is also a temporal sovereign? Does this imply that the Catholic's patriotism is not entire but divided? Apart from the official doctrinal response to this charge by ecclesiastical authorities, there is an objective approach, that is to say, a consideration which transcends or cuts across religious lines, namely, the status accorded to the Holy See in international law by the practice of states.

States which in their public law grant preferential status to different faiths—Protestant, Catholic, Islamic, Oriental—and states which profess religious neutrality have for decades recognized the Holy See to be a general, permanent and perfect subject of international law. As such the Holy See has *in its own capacity* always enjoyed the rights of active and passive legation and concluded agreements (concordats) with states. In addition, the Holy See can conclude normal international treaties on behalf of her temporalities, before 1870 for the Papal State, and since 1929 for the City of the Vatican. The unique status of the Holy See in general international law consists in the fact that it is precisely as a spiritual sovereign that she enjoys the rights of sovereignty ordinarily accorded to national political sovereignty and that no other Church or religion has known the same status in the world community of states.

Sovereignty and international personality is vested with the Holy See precisely as a spiritual authority, independently of the existence of a papal state. From 1870 to 1929 when she was without territories her unique status remained unchanged and she continued to exercise her customary rights in international law. The reason for the existence of the State of Vatican City is wholly derivative and contingent upon the presupposition that the free exercise of a supranational spiritual sovereignty by the Holy See is better ensured by an independent territorial jurisdiction of its own. Prior to 1870 and subsequent to 1929, there have been two subjects of international law, the Papal States, or the State of Vatican City, and the Holy See. The pope united in his own person these two distinct subjects of international law, and of the two obviously the more important and primary is that of the Holy See. Papal nuncios and apostolic delegates are accredited by the Holy See, not by the papal state. Diplomatic relations by the states of England, Netherlands, Finland, Japan, Egypt, India, Indonesia, and others are established with the Holy See and not, as is popularly supposed, with the Papal State. Their diplomatic representatives are accredited to the spiritual sovereignty and not to the temporal jurisdiction. None of these states suffers any qualms about divided allegiance or contrary allegiances and it is patently absurd to suppose that their diplomatic relations with the Holy See import a confessional bias.

What then precisely is the significance of the state of Vatican City? A study comparing it with the Holy See may make this clear. Both of them are subjects of general international law. The Holy See is a nonterritorial international personality; Vatican City is a territorial international personality. The Holy See is not a state but it exercises sovereign prerogatives, including sovereignty over the Vatican State. Some writers on international law call Vatican City a "vassal" state. It is not autonomous, its existence is wholly derivative, and it is subordinate to and subserves the purposes of the Holy See. Even as a territorial personality, Vatican City is wanting as a state, for it does not meet the Greek requirement of self-sufficiency. There are no industrial, agricultural or commercial enterprises that could sustain an economy. Actually, the state of the Vatican City, and for that matter, of the Holy See is almost wholly dependent for its financial resources upon worldwide contributions of its faithful for maintenance and administration. Furthermore, it barely fulfills the Roman law requirement of territorial definition and a coterminous jurisdiction. Because of its small size and because its activities and purposes are totally different from those of national political states, it does not enjoy membership as a state in the United Nations. Its constitution derives wholly from the necessity of the Holy See to be independent and free from any political domination. The spiritual office of all papal representatives is symbolically attested to by the honorary precedence that they enjoy in the diplomatic corp over all political diplomats.

International law does not, of course, commit itself to any theological position. Its recognition of the non-territorial international personality of the Holy See precisely as a spiritual sovereign cannot be construed as having any confessional implication whatever. That being so, we may add that Catholic ecclesiology, which understandably is not acceptable to non-Catholics, should be reassuring to them on this matter. The pope or bishop of Rome is acknowledged by Catholics to be the Vicar of Christ on earth. In virtue of the apostolic succession the Roman pontiff exercises a primacy of jurisdiction over all the bishops and over all the faithful. His jurisdiction extends not only to faith and morals, but also to those matters which pertain to the discipline and law of the Church throughout the world. It is clearly necessary that the Holy See enjoy complete immunity from the influence, dictation, or interference of any national political sovereignty in the exercise of its spiritual authority over its faithful who are citizens of different national governments throughout the world. In matters touching upon faith and morals, the pope is never a foreigner. Wherever the Catholic faithful are, there too is the pope as Vicar of Christ, present by the universal extension of his divinely invested spiritual office.

Now there are non-Catholics who readily admit to the purely spiritual allegiance of Catholics to the Holy See but who fear that this may be the very vehicle through which papal or hierarchial influence or "pressure" may be exerted upon the religious conscience of a Catholic in the exercise of his presidential duties. This fear is emphasized by the difference between the dominance that Protestant theology gives to private judgment as the ordinary guide of conscience and the deference which Catholics ordinarily and normally show to the authoritative direction of the Church. The difficulty is further confounded by the misconception about the extent of papal authority, which is considered to be so absolute and complete that a Catholic president would be inhibited in making any independent political judgments by an apparent conflict of the two allegiances. One would think that John Henry Newman had disposed of this lingering ghost by his reply to the identical allegations of Mr. Gladstone:

When, then, Mr. Gladstone asks Catholics how they can obey the Queen and yet obey the Pope, since it may happen that the commands of the two authorities may clash, I answer that it is my *rule,* both to obey the one and to obey the other, but that there is no rule in this world without exceptions, and if either the Pope or the Queen demanded of men an "absolute obedience" he or she would be transgressing the laws of human nature and human society. I give an absolute obedience to neither. Further, if ever this double allegiance pulled me in contrary ways, which in this age of the world I think it never will, then I should decide according to the particular case, which is beyond all rule, and must be decided on its merits. I should look to see what theologians could do for me, what the bishops and clergy around me, what my confessor; what my friends whom I revered; and if, after all, I could not take their view of the matter, then I must rule myself by my own judgment and my own conscience.

And in another place in the same letter:

The Pope's infallibility indeed and his supreme authority have in the Vatican *capita* been declared matters of faith; but his prerogative of infallibility lies in matters speculative, and his prerogative of authority is no infallibility, in laws, commands, or measures. His infallibility bears upon the domain of thought, not directly of action, and while it may fairly exercise the theologian, philosopher, or man of science, it scarcely concerns the politician.

All moral obligations descend from God. A reasonable person will generally in difficult cases consult those invested with the proper authority and competence to ascertain the correct course of action. To be bound in conscience is to be bound by one's own conscience. That is not to say that it is a self-imposed obligation. Rather it is the free personal acknowledgment of what ought to be done.

Almost all theologians and political philosophers hold that the province of faith is that of the Church and that politics is the proper domain of the state. Almost all agree that morality is the common concern of both jurisdictions because man as citizen and believer acts as a moral agent. This provides the potential source of conflict and friction between the two authorities, religious and secular, and it may be attributed not so much to the mutual denial of jurisdiction as to the priority and extent of its exercise.

The objectives of civil society are eminently moral: social justice, public order, security, peace, the legal protection of natural rights which it is not in the power of the state to deny or abrogate, such as the right to religious freedom. The distinction between positive law and morality is that of a part to the whole. The performance of a human act is always under the jurisdiction of the universal moral law. The problem arises in the pluralist interpretation and opposing application of the moral law to an action of public law. Political authority may not shirk its responsibilities in assisting the moral life of its subjects and yet on the other hand should not arbitrarily impose one moral philosophy rather than another upon its citizens. Reason would require that the political authorities should expect and welcome the efforts of all duly constituted religious authorities such as the Board of Rabbis, the Protestant Council of Churches, and the Catholic Bishops, as well as private citizens to express themselves on grave moral questions affecting the public order as becomes their duty. In turn the public at large has the right to weigh the justice and reasonableness of these authoritative pronouncements, with sensitive regard for the rights of all consciences and the exigencies of public order. Where contrary and conflicting positions are affirmed then public discussion and debate should proceed on the basis of reason and with an appeal to reason. The natural law, which is the law of human nature and not the law of men, offers the most optimistic possibility for civilized men to discourse their way to agreement. The natural law remains unalterably the unitive bond of all men of different faiths, and at the same time the proper context in which to view the legitimate role of public power. I take the source of the difficulty to be generally a flight from reason, the fear that an agreement might be reached which the absolutist dissenter might be required to respect.

Now on the American scene three specific issues are raised about the Catholic in the White House: provisions for a birth control program in a foreign aid bill, diplomatic relations with the Holy See, and federal aid to all publicly accredited schools, including of religious schools.

It is the unique genius of the American Constitution that it guarantees the exercise of religious freedom for the president of the United States without thereby impairing the operations of the political process or imposing forcibly by virtue of presidential authority his moral conscience upon others. Should a Catholic president, then, in response to his moral convictions about birth control, refuse to approve it, the congressional bill might still become law automatically without his signature after the passage of the constitutionally prescribed time or by congressional action overriding the veto. Every presidential action must always be viewed within the context of the political process. One might add, too, a *sotto voce* reflection that obedience to one's own personal conscience is not always and necessarily in conformity with the publicly avowed dictates of its religious profession. Not every Quaker public officer subscribes to pacifism.

Federal aid to religious schools and formal diplomatic relations with the Holy See are nonreligious questions. They are political decisions dependent upon congressional action which is sensitively respondent to the public and ultimately subject to judicial review. No one may reasonably *insist* that there *must* be formal diplomatic relations with the Holy See. But to insist that they must never be established at any event for any reason may well conceal a symbolic affront to Catholics not unlike that shown to this day to a Catholic presidential candidate. The practice of Protestant,

Buddhist, Hindu, Moslem states with legally established religions and of states with separation of Church and State contradicts the misconception that formal diplomatic relations with the Holy See imply a preferential status for one Church or discrimination against other Churches.

Our second consideration is about the alleged incompatibility of the philosophical and religious dogmatism of Catholicism and political democracy. The common Protestant assumption is that Luther and the Reformation brought freedom into the world, that American liberty is a late product of the Reformation of the same type as those liberties so loudly advertised on the European continent by anti-Catholic liberals throughout the nineteenth century. Hence it can be an occasion of sincere and agreeable surprise to discover that the American Catholic can be loyal to his country. This assumption is uncritical and wholly gratuitous because it is invalid both historically and sociologically. The freedoms proclaimed by Luther and spread by the Reformation may not be isolated from the theological and political syntheses of the various Protestant theories: justification by faith, the servile will, the debased value of human reason, the concentration in the sovereign of all external powers even where ecclesiastical matters were concerned imply rather politico-religious intolerance and a rigid religious-political structure of communities. Luther and Calvin were logical when they maintained the right of banishing or burning heretics, sectarians, and all those who by denying one of the dogmas resulting from the common interpretation of the Bible denied at the same time the new Christian society and the basis of social power. As for the American experience we should not blithely forget that many of our colonial immigrants fled from persecution in Protestant State-Church establishments of the old world and that they in turn persecuted religious dissenters in the new world. The historical process leading to religious toleration has other theoretical and historical roots than Protestantism.

The rational misconception derives from the false juxtaposition of two different levels of human experience as though the relation between the two—and related they are—was of an arithmetic or geometric proportion. It is argued that philosophical and religious dogmatism engenders habits of intolerance for what is believed to be false, and is therefore conducive to political absolutism and civil intolerance. Such an equation misconstrues as equivalent the ends and purposes of religious and civil life. Man is determined as to his end and indeterminate as to the means for realizing his end. It is the rightful province of theologians and philosophers to ascertain the meaning of human existence and to yield intellectual assent to conclusive evidence. They are free to inquire but not free to fashion man's destiny. It is the proper domain of statesmen to contrive apt means and multiple courses of action from which a choice may be made for the governance of the civil order, ever mindful and respectful of the religious conscience of its subjects. Dogmatism in any science is an intellectual achievement; it is the goal toward which all learning strives and upon whose certainties rest the possibilities of a life of convenience without fear. For example, dogmatism in the natural sciences, instead of shutting us in on every hand, constitutes the means at our disposal for acting upon things and for obtaining power over them. A knowledge of the laws of things enables us to control them; consequently instead of checking our freedom, natural physical laws make it efficacious. Religious dogmatism frees us from the phantom world of blind fate and the mythical world of demons by assuring us that we are children of God, for whose sake the world of forces and life has been created. Philosophical dogmatism tells us that men have been created equal by God and that therefore no one has by nature a right to govern another, save by his consent. Historically, revolutions for political freedom have been fought by men who were willing to sacrifice their possessions and their lives for their beliefs. Conversely, theological and philosophical skepticism and relativism deprive a people of the spiritual and intellectual resources with which to withstand the pretensions of the omnicompetent state. As modern history only too patently proves, the totalitarian state steps into this intellectual vacuum and makes the arrogant claim to dogmatize (with force, if necessary) not only politically but theologically and philosophically as well. If the theologians and philosophers cannot be validly sure of the meaning of human existence then how can anyone be sure that Marxism is an error? What would be the sense of fighting it at so great a sacrifice? Dogma is not only the prize achievement of human intelligence; it is also the condition for a free society.

The third consideration focuses on the fears that many Protestants have about a numerically superior Catholic electorate. Might it not be tempted to change the Constitution to restrict the religious freedom of non-Catholics? The source of these fears, European history, past and present, and our own colonial period, is creditable to neither side. Broadly speaking, there have been in both religious camps two traditions on Church-State relations. The major tradition would have public law confer a preferential status to the "true" religion and civil restrictions upon or civil tolerance for the dissenters. The minor tradition affirms that civil society is an exigency of the divine natural law and that it prescinds from the prerogatives of revelational theology. It maintains that both religious and secular empowerments are each independent of the other and superior in their own proper domain. It is forced to recognize that there are certain common areas of morality wherein both jurisdictions converge, which provide the potential source of conflict as well as the occasion of harmonious cooperation. In America the minor tradition has gradually emerged as the major one, for Catholics and Protestants alike, in the post-Civil War period.

The Catholic record in American history beginning with Lord Baltimore's Act of Toleration of 1649 and continuing to this day is remarkably reassuring. The Catholic hierarchy, since the days of Bishop John Carroll, has without exception repeatedly professed great devotion to and grateful appreciation of the American Constitution, particularly the religious clauses of the First Amendment. Catholics as private citizens and in public office have given no cause for us to doubt their patriotism. In matters political, there is no instance of an ecclesiastical call for Catholic political solidarity. Catholics in both Houses of Congress do not vote *en bloc*. And in surveys of state and municipal elections there is no consistent pattern that large concentrations of Catholic voters are committed to Catholic candidates. Catholic political solidarity is a myth.

But what of a Catholic bloc vote understood as a conscientious response to a religious position on a public law issue such as birth control and sterilization? Such controversies are inevitable wherever there is religious pluralism and the possibility of a bloc vote involves Protestant and Jew no less than Catholic. Now the political process of democratic society settles public issues through the presumably reasonable procedure of majority decision. In the rational and tentative expectation that the formal reason for the numerical majority be outside itself—in reason—this procedure, subject to review and reversal, allows for peaceful change and progress while at the same time it serves to express corporate capacity and responsibility. If then a group, religious or not, should express the solidarity of its convictions through the voting process, this is the expectation or hazard, if you will, inherent in the process of arriving at majority decision. The problem incumbent upon all is so to condition this democratic process that there does not ensue an arbitrary majority rule over a minority. The only possible way of resolving this dilemma in a rational manner is by recourse, through reason, to the unitive bond of the divine natural law which is the law of man and not of men. Doctrinal positions are generally affirmed authoritatively from opposing camps. Despite the agreement about the necessity and desirability of intercredal dialogue there is not in evidence as much collective and cooperative discussion as is needed. Round table discussions by theologians, philosophers, statesmen, which prescind without disavowing religious dogmas, might inquire into the moral laws of human nature and ascertain what, in the political order, would be in accord with them. Such collective thinking might reveal that there is much more substance than shadow in the natural law and, further, might provide the political authorities with that general consensus which legislation should recognize. What of the obdurate and exceptional dissenter? It is a strange pathology of modern politics that it abhors the absolute dictator, totalitarian democracy, majoritarian rule but cannot place in proper perspective the absolutist dissenter.

In conclusion may I suggest that a Catholic candidate for the presidency might choose, even at the cost of votes, not to confine himself to a series of disclaimers on hypothetical issues. He might take a more positive approach and explain how his Catholic Faith would enrich his subjective dispositions in the performance of public duties. He might, without embarrassment, point to papal teaching on social justice, on the social responsibilities of labor and capital not only to one another but also to the community at large, on the principle of subsidiarity which Pope Pius XI opposed to the monolithic state. He might call attention to the contributions of Pope Pius XII on international relations and institutions. He might explain how his faith encourages foreign aid for deeper reasons than expediency. He might explain that the opposition between Catholicism and Communism is profoundly theological and humanist; he might point out papal teaching on the necessity of never acknowledging as final the captivity of certain peoples. He might point to the remarkable agreement of certain central Catholic dogmas with the American Declaration of Independence, how the Church insists on the moral basis for education, patriotism, the fulfillment of all civic duties. The Catholic conception of the social order supports and promotes legislation for the betterment of labor conditions, of housing facilities, for economic provisions for the aged and the needy. All of these and many others are not exclusively Catholic doctrines but nonetheless Catholic they are and they should inspire the faithful in the promotion of a better and a more expansive life for the whole community. If a Catholic candidate for president is challenged on matters of his Faith then he might welcome the opportunity to make it better known and perhaps better understood. Surely, one would suppose that the historical record of over two centuries would disclose convincing and conclusive evidence of the patriotism of the Catholic, his devotion to the laws of his country, and his full share of sacrifice in her behalf.

Psychoanalysis and Christianity

Emilio Dido, Ph.D.*

Psychopathology should certainly be included among the sciences which have greatly benefited from the extraordinary progress realized by humanity during the past century. Many scholars have contributed towards the development of this science, but the most decisive and ingenious contribution undoubtedly is that of Sigmund Freud.

It is true that his contribution has been greatly controverted, but it is difficult to deny that Freud has given to psychopathology a new and more constructive orientation. His psychoanalytical method has produced results which could never have been attained within the framework of traditional psychology.

For an objective evaluation of Freud's achievements, one must disentangle his scientific works from his

* Dr. Dido received his doctorate in philosophy from the Catholic University of the Sacred Heart, Milan. He studied and worked with Father Augustine Gemelli, O.F.M., who developed the world renowned laboratory of experimental psychology at the Catholic University of the Sacred Heart in Milan.

erroneous philosophy. Freud's skill and qualifications in the field of psychopathology are as unquestionable as his incompetence in philosophy.

Just as Aristotle's erroneous physics does not invalidate his metaphysics, however, so neither does Freud's spurious philosophy invalidate his scientific conquests. Assuming that the basic elements of Freudian psychopathology are valid, these elements should stand up to the testing by logic and rational psychology. In fact, the assimilation of the psychoanalytical method into traditional Catholic philosophy cannot help but strengthen the efficacy of the method itself.

The limited scope of this article does not permit us to discuss Freudian philosophy or to explain at length the fundamentals of psychoanalysis; we will limit ourselves to pointing out the most significant elements and achievements of psychoanalysis and to evaluating them within the light of the Catholic faith.

From the technical point of view, psychoanalysis should be considered a "method of science" rather than a "science." On the other hand, along with his new method and as a foundation for it, Freud also gave us an original psychology.

Freudian psychology is quite different from the traditional, at least in its terminology and in its mechanism. According to Freud, there are three psychological coefficients constituting the human personality: the Id, the Ego and the Superego. These are the three active components of his anthropological system. The makeup of our personal individuality depends entirely on the dosage of these three psychic ingredients.

The Id is the expression of all that is irrational in human nature, and it includes the instincts of the species, the inherited qualities, and in general all the urges which drive a living being toward the fulfillment of its biological life. The Id also includes all the urges derived from patterns of action or habits which human beings have learned through imitation or by adaptation to their environment. Its principle functions are to unify, develop and protect our physical life, to avoid pain, and particularly to satisfy the general desires of sensitive pleasure.

The main function of the Ego is to maintain the total unity of the personality—to harmonize the internal pressure of the Id with the resistance or the demands of external circumstances. In other words, the Ego is the principle of stability; the ruling part of the human being which directs and coordinates both stimuli and inhibitory forces. Its ultimate goal is to accomplish the maximum possible gratification of all the needs of the individual. Freudians would say that the Ego is the person, but this word has been used in so many different meanings that it has become equivocal.

The Superego is not something originally existing in us, as is "reason," for example, which we potentially possess from the beginning and eventually develop through usage. The Superego is rather a psychic superstructure, something injected into our psychology by parents, teachers, traditions, by the social environment in which we were born and brought up. Nevertheless,

Freud does not exclude some hereditary influences. The Superego is sometimes referred to as conscience—the moral criterion of evil and good, our subjective evaluation of deeds and thoughts. Its main function is to merge the individual into organized society, to harmonize our personal life with the life of society; it is the inner moral censor of our social life.

From the above description of the Superego, it is obvious that it cannot be conceived of as a faculty or as an entity but only as a converging of forces, namely, as a psychological resultant including all the moral and esthetic principles which the individual received from his social environment. Finally, it should be emphasized that the Id, Ego, and Superego are not to be considered as three separate factors but rather as three different functions of the human psychic mechanism. Let us now analyze these three components of Freudian psychology.

Substantially, there are no serious objections against the Id. We cannot really say that the Id is an original discovery of modern psychology, but we can accept it as a convenient term to unify all the feelings connoting biological needs. The critical conclusions regarding the Ego and Superego are quite different. When the Ego is presented as the ruling part of the human being, we immediately think of the will and its functions. On the other hand, the description of the Superego as arbiter of our moral conscience reminds us of reason or of the practical intellect of St. Thomas. Nothing, however, is more antithetic to the Freudian conception of Ego and Superego than the scholastic doctrine of intellect and will. A brief comparison of these two systems will demonstrate their absolute irreducibility. For the purpose of clarity, we will compare the two positions by coupling "Will and Ego" and "Intellect and Superego."

Will and Ego

According to Thomistic philosophy, the essential characteristic of the will is freedom and it is precisely because of this quality that the will is distinguished from the animal appetite. The will is a *spiritual* faculty and its law is auto-determination; that is to say, it is free. The animal appetite is a sensitive faculty and it reacts mechanically in conformity with biological laws. Free will is the foundation of all moral laws and without it man would be exempt from any moral responsibility. The Freudian Ego, on the contrary, is not at all a deliberating faculty but only a sort of network which balances all the different reactions of the human being. Obviously, in this conception there is no room for freedom; in fact, the Ego is determined by the result of the spontaneous combinations and interactions of the forces operating in the individual. We might say the Ego mechanically does that which can be mechanically done. For example, let us suppose that a stimulus from the Id urges an individual to perform a certain action of which the Superego or censor disapproves. In this case, the function of the Ego is: first, to make these two antagonistic forces collide until either the Id or the Superego gains the upper hand; secondly, to carry out the urge of the winner according to the possibilities offered by the external environment. If the winner should be the Superego, the function of the Ego would be to inhibit the urge of the Id.

The human intellect, because of its spiritual nature, has the capacity to penetrate and grasp the essence of things, to know things objectively as they are in themselves—in other words, to attain "truth." Thus, because of our intellect, we are able to define things with universal formulas. For example, the circle is defined as a plane figure bounded by a curved line every point of which is equally distant from the center. This formula is valid for all possible circles regardless of size. We define man as a rational animal, which means that the human being is a composition of spiritual and animal nature; again, this formula is valid for all men in all times. Furthermore, by means of reason we know the laws which govern and rule the practical life of man, laws which are neither arbitrary nor conventional but which stem from the same human nature. In other words, moral law is to man as biological law is to the animal and physical laws are to bodies. Two plus two is four not because we state it; rather, we state it because in reality it cannot be anything but four. So also, to kill, to steal, to lie, to curse and so on are evil actions not because society condemns them, but rather they are condemned by society because they really are evil actions.

We frequently fail, certainly, in the arduous task of seeking the truth because original sin wounded human nature and weakened both our intellect and will. This does not mean, however, that truth does not exist or that everything is relative and arbitrary. Truth is susceptible of development, and errors can be corrected, but what is true is true and remains so forever. The Freudian Superego, on the contrary, is nothing other than a mass of regulations and norms stuffed into our minds by the social environment, rules and norms which were entirely and arbitrarily produced by society and, hence, completely without objective foundation. Granted that we do assimilate the precepts which regulate our moral life from the environment in which we live, this is not sufficient reason for declaring them arbitrary and conventional. From the teaching of society we also assimilate mathematical precepts, and yet no one ever thought that this was a reason for invalidating their objectivity. To conclude this comparative analysis of the Thomistic and Freudian doctrines regarding the structure of human psychology we may now synthesize the two doctrines, respectively, as follows:

On the one hand we have the intellect, which provides universal and immutable moral principles, while the Freudian Superego provides changeable and arbitrary ones. On the other hand, we have the Thomistic "will" which is essentially free by nature and the Freudian Ego which acts in an absolutely deterministic fashion. At this point some may ask: if Freud's psychology is so erroneous, what then is his contribution toward the development of this science? The answer is that Freud contributed toward the progress of psychopathology, not of rational psychology. The first is an empirical science while the second is a speculative science. All the discoveries of the brilliant Viennese psychiatrist belong in the field of psychic phenomenology; therefore their validity is of a positive order, not of a rational or dialectical order.

Before presenting the salient elements and the achievement of psychoanalysis, it seemed expedient to compare briefly the two psychologies—Thomistic and Freudian—and to point out the incongruity of the latter. This will enable us to avoid the danger of confusion.

Repression

As Freud himself has stated: The cornerstone of psychoanalysis is *repression*. But fully to understand the meaning and the value of this concept, we must first analyze the mechanism of consciousness in its various degrees and stratifications. In fact, according to Freud, the possibility of understanding the psychic phenomenology of both normal and abnormal behavior depends entirely upon our knowledge of the mechanism of the conscious.

The conscious has three stages: the conscious, the preconscious, and the unconscious. The concept of *conscious* is used in psychoanalysis to unify and express all the experiences of our daily life of which we are *actually aware*. Therefore it includes emotions, feelings, thoughts, reminiscences. It should be stressed, however, that they belong in the field of the conscious only when they are actually present in our mind, that is, when we are aware of them.

The preconscious comprises all the psychological

material which has already been in our conscious. Freud places into the preconscious all those thoughts, feelings, and desires which were and can be in the conscious, although they are not at this moment. Hence the preconscious is a potential conscious. From it we may recall, although with some effort, all that we need and recognize it as our own.

But the most original concept of psychoanalysis is that of the *unconscious*. The striking consequences and conclusions which Freud derived from it opened new and vast horizons to him. The unconscious enabled him to explain a notable number of psychic phenomena which had not yet been given a satisfactory explanation.

To give an exact definition of the unconscious is rather a problem, for Freud was a great observer but a poor philosopher. Furthermore, he was not systematic and his works are always disorganized and vague. Nevertheless, we will try to formulate an approximate description of this essential Freudian theory.

As suggested by the word itself, the unconscious consists in latent energies operating within us of which we are not aware. These energies summing up or intersecting one another affect our behavior in different ways; since we do not have any experience of them we can become aware of their existence only indirectly, namely, by their effects. These hidden psychic energies are the manifestation and product of what Freud calls *repression*. *Repression* must not be confused with *suppression*.

Suppression is always a *voluntary* inhibition. It is an inhibitory operation performed by the Ego under the pressure of either the Superego or of the Id. This voluntary inhibition or suppression is always the result of a psychic conflict between Id and Superego.

For instance, if an urge of the Id is disapproved by a sanction of the Superego which carries a greater quantity of psychic energy, then the Ego suppresses the urge of the Id. Evidently we have the opposite result when the psychic energy of the Id is greater than that of the censor—Superego. Since suppression is a voluntary operation, it obviously belongs in the field of conscious; hence we are always *aware* of it.

As of now, we have only considered cases where psychic conflicts were solved with the total suppression of the weaker force, where the Ego, affected and determined either by the Id or Superego, entirely inhibited the weaker urge. However, it frequently happens that the difference between the two intersecting forces is not sufficient to allow such decisive results. In such cases, the Ego, although affected by the prevailing element, does not succeed in completely inhibiting the conflicting urge. At this point, Freud introduces his concept of repression.

When a wish is only *partially* inhibited, namely, when the Ego suppresses it enough to hinder its fulfillment but not enough to exhaust its charge of psychic energy, this wish is transformed into an undercurrent force which remains completely outside our awareness. We have here all the elements of the mechanism of repression. Repression is a failure of suppression—a frustrated but not exhausted urge. This urge will continue to exist in a state of repression in the unconscious. We will not have any direct knowledge of it and yet the repressed wish may disturb our peace of mind by producing complexes and may attain some gratification through our dreams. In the most severe cases, repression may have very serious consequences including all forms of mental disorder from neurosis to schizophrenia.

As we have suggested, the ordinary outlet of the unconscious is the dream. The dream, says Freud, is the disguised fulfillment of a repressed wish. During sleep the conscious is much less active than during the waking state; this allows the repressed wishes to obtain some gratification. In order to make this gratification less offensive and more acceptable to the Superego, the condemned urge is usually disguised.

According to Freud, then, all dreams are meaningful but their meaning does not coincide with the manifest contents of the dream. The real meaning and cause of the dream is the latent content, that is the repressed wish of the unconscious. The disguise often makes it very difficult to discover the latent content of the dream and only the cooperation of the patient and the skill of the psychoanalyst makes it possible to bring the repressed wish back from the unconscious to the conscious.

This doctrine of dreams plays a primary role in psychoanalysis. In fact, it is principally through analysis and interpretation of dreams that the psychoanalyst sounds the hidden recesses of the unconscious and brings to light the psychic elements of repressed conflicts. This achievement is particularly effective and important in the psychoanalytical therapy of mental disorders.

Freud stresses that mental disorders are always due to psychic conflicts and repression; to cure such patients therefore one must bring back into their conscious the knowledge of the repressed wish which has been the cause of their illness.

Another important means employed by psychoanalysis to explore the unconscious of the patient is the technique of *free association*. Here the patient is requested to lie down and relax on a couch in order to reproduce as closely as possible the condition of the dream. This complete relaxation and removal of all mental inhibition is supposed to reduce all forms of repression. The patient is then asked to relate to the psychoanalyst everything that comes to his mind with absolute freedom and indiscrimination, including minor details, trivial facts and painful thoughts.

Interpretation of dreams and free association are not to be used as two separate methods of analysis; on the contrary, they should complement and integrate each other. These two methods, when skillfully employed, will enable the psychoanalyst to explore thoroughly and to unveil the unconscious of the patient. Guided and enlightened by the psychoanalyst, the patient will rediscover those painful experiences of his childhood which his mechanism of defense had buried in the forgetfulness of the unconscious. However, the revival of the repressed material is often impeded by what Freud calls *resistance*. Resistance is an automatic and involuntary reaction—the wall of protection for repression.

The most typical and classical form of resistance occurs when the repression is due to a moral conflict. Let us analyze one of the many cases reported by Freud.

CASE: A young girl disturbed by an obsessional neurosis has the habit of frequently running into her room, locking the door, and then opening the window. She is able neither to give an explanation for this behavior nor to check it. Psychoanalysis interprets this apparently bizarre pattern of action as a typical case of a repressed sexual complex which has been displaced because of a failure of suppression. The analysis confirmed the interpretation.

The girl used to entertain impure thoughts produced by the Id. Later the development of her moral conscience—Superego—impelled the Ego to reject and repress these impure thoughts, which were buried in the unconscious. After a while, new circumstances, identified by the analysis, intervened to modify the equilibrium in favor of the Id and the repressed impure thoughts were then de-repressed. In other words, the strengthening of the Id allowed some return from the unconscious to the conscious of the repressed material. The Superego, however, impelled the Ego to compromise, to disguise these impure thoughts lest they be too offensive to the Superego. The closing of the door signified the inhibition of the impure thoughts and this satisfied the Superego; conversely the opening of the window signified the welcoming of the impure thoughts, but in a symbolic, disguised form which in some ways satisfied the Id, without offending the censor. This process is similar to the technique used by the unconscious in dreams, and it is generally suggested by a dream. On the other hand, the process of analysis is therapeutically efficacious only when the psychoanalyst succeeds in depressing the unconscious, namely, when the repression, unshackled from the straitjacket of resistance, returns to the field of the conscious. In the case discussed the role of the analyst is to lead the girl to discover the real meaning of her obsessional behavior. In order to carry out this challenging task, the analyst should succeed in bringing the patient to break through the barrier of resistance.

Resistance is always a psychological blindness; a psychic device which automatically prevents the revival of the forgotten material. Resistance blocks the return into the field of the conscious of those repressed thoughts or feelings which would once again enkindle the conflict. This task is, above all, the real challenge for the psychoanalyst.

It sometimes happens that the de-repression has the effect of restoring the original psychic conflict, in which case the psychoanalyst does not have any guarantee that the patient will be able to solve the conflict better than previously. In this instance the remedy will be worse than the illness itself.

For example, in the above mentioned case, the girl found in her obsession a compromise solution for the distressing conflict. The problem is to know how the patient will react when she is once again confronted with the conflict of impure thoughts. Will she yield or will she suppress them? At this point the case is no longer a purely psychological problem but also a moral one.

If the girl is not willing to sacrifice the gratification of her sexual feelings in their disguised form, she will not be able to overcome the resistance. On the other hand, even if in spite of this attitude she managed to overcome the resistance, this would only contribute to the deterioration of her moral and spiritual condition. In fact, she could substitute for the disguised satisfaction of her sexual feelings an open gratification of them; that is, she could pass from an unconscious moral compromise to a conscious immorality.

From these considerations it becomes evident that such patients can be normalized only if they are willing to subject the Id to the Superego which we call conscience. Is this always possible? It is. With the assistance of divine grace and good will it is always possible for us to attain justice and to overcome what Freud calls "libido" and Christians call concupiscence.

However, it should be stressed that divine grace and good will alone do not cure neurosis, much less psychosis. God can certainly perform miracles and sometimes He does, but ordinarily He governs the universe through ordinary means. Hence mental disorders should normally be cured by the means offered to us by science. Mental disorders belong to a special type of malady, a type all its own. As Freud pointed out, these illnesses are always due to a psychic conflict. Although the presence of some anatomical or physiological anomaly is generally presupposed, the efficient cause is always of a psychological order. Unfortunately, Freud did not have any notion of rational psychology and this prevented him from seeing the full value and the ultimate consequences of his discovery.

In the Freudian conception, "man" is none other than the result of the evolutionary process of a purely material reality. If Freud had recognized the spiritual soul he would have seen that psychological recovery is not always simply a clinical problem; frequently it is or may become a moral problem also. Freud insists that the problem of psychoanalysis is the restoration of mental health and not moral re-education. We claim that mental disorder is often caused by *moral* disorder.

Original sin upset the harmony which governed creation and aroused in man a constitutional conflict which is certainly moral in nature.

"I do not the good that I wish, but the evil that I do not wish I perform." These words of St. Paul vividly express the intrinsic conflict which torments every human being. It is a conflict between good and evil, light and darkness, justice and injustice. To enable man to overcome this conflict, the Son of God died on the cross. But, His sacrifice becomes effective only for those who have at least a minimum of good will. And man's will is good only when it conforms itself, at least intentionally, with God's will. It is God's will that we be perfect and that in order to achieve our perfection we use all the means, natural and supernatural, offered to us by Providence.

Hence, it is His will that man pray and ask for all his needs, and frequent the sacraments. It is also His will that one go to a physician when ill and why not to a psychoanalyst when mentally disturbed? However, if prudence requires that we should solve our human problems without neglecting these natural means, we must also recall the words of warning pronounced by Christ in the solemn intimacy of the Last Supper: *Sine me nihil potestis facere* (Without me you can do nothing).

Evolution and Catholic Theology

REV. J. FRANKLIN EWING, S.J.*

E VOLUTION, thy name is Confusion! This might well be the exclamation of the average Catholic, who has not had time to become an expert in any of the various aspects of the problem of evolution.

This confusion is helped along by a great many people. For example, there are the cartoonists. Not only do they do such unrealistic things as depict primitive man assailing dinosaurs, but they still show the cave man, equipped with a club, dragging a female off to his cave by the hair of the head. They still do this, in spite of the fact, as Chesterton remarked many, many years ago, that scientists who invaded the caves to dig up ancient man did not find a row of female skulls all cracked like eggs. Instead, they found tools and paint-

* Father Ewing is associate professor of anthropology at Fordham University as well as director of the Institute of Mission Studies. He is also a fellow of the *American Anthropological Association* and a fellow of the *American Association for the Advancement of Science*. He received the *Médaille pour la mérite Lebanon* 1940 for palaeontological work in that country.

ings on the cave walls. Obviously, one thing they could never find would be fossilized customs which dictated exactly how men should act towards women!

The newspapers further confuse us. They feature new discoveries, each discovery equipped with a more complicated name than the one before it. They also help us out by stating in a headline every so often that Darwinism has been overthrown again.

Articles by anthropologists and biologists add to the confusion by advocating the application of rigorous evolutionary thought to human affairs, and away with such "primitive" concepts as religion, the soul, and the dignity of man.

We observe, too, the extreme reserve that many priests and religious have toward the theory of evolution in any shape or form. At the same time, we are assured by all biologists that evolution is a "fact." Can anyone blame a Catholic who has not specialized in this field for being confused?

We propose to attack this confusion first of all by trying to pare away the fundamental distracting excrescences that have grown up around the phenomena of biological evolution. We are discussing only the evolution of man because this is what interests people most.

Secondly, we shall very briefly state the present Catholic theological attitude towards the evolution of man. Fortunately, this can be done much more succinctly.

Thirdly, we shall briefly discuss the potentialities of evolution for the Catholic life of mind and heart.

Once again, we must make a distinction which has

been emphasized in many previous publications. This distinction is that of the levels of knowledge. Catholics, in the great tradition of Western thought, realize that there is a difference between what the scientist can learn and know, what a philosopher can learn or know, and what a theologian can achieve. The scientist deals with material reality. The great (and nowadays sometimes terrifying) successes of science have been achieved by the scientist acting *as if he were* a materialist. He observes material facts, correlates them, and forms hypotheses and theories about them. His laboratory work should be preceded by hypotheses so that he can attempt to ask intelligent questions of nature. But his primary result is the description of the "How?" of nature.

Thus, the physicist tells us how electrons and atoms and gravitation work. The biologist tells us how cells and chromosomes and evolution work. The social scientist tells us how the customs and thoughts of mankind work.

The philosopher, on the other hand, applies to the data of human experience the process of reflective analysis. He attempts to get down to the "Why?" of things. He deals with essences, with the reasons for processes. Hence, the philosopher can talk about the fact of the human soul. The scientist cannot.

The pre-eminent source of knowledge for Catholics is revelation. Here we have the actual word of God about reality. True, this word is not concerned with the "How" of the universe (except as it involves the why). For the Catholic, there can never be any question of a direct opposition of revelation and science or philosophy. But if there should seem to be such an opposition, then revelation takes precedence. It may happen, in human experience, that we do not fully understand revelation with regard to a certain point. It may also happen that the fullness of our life in Christ and in the Church may be aided very much by developments in science and philosophy. It is certainly true that the more we know about reality, the better we can know and love God and His revelation. It is also true that there could never be any opposition between any other form of experience and revelation.

There are not too many excrescences in the realm of science that we need discuss. The situation, as we shall see, will be quite different when we discuss what some scientists have had to say about evolution, with reference to philosophy or theology.

However, let us register a protest against a very common remark among scientists. This remark is: "Evolution is a fact." One would do better to reserve the word "fact" for a phenomenon which is observable. It is a fact that water boils at 212 degrees Fahrenheit. This is a fact of observation, if one wishes to make a distinction. But to label a conclusion or deduction a "fact" seems dangerous.

Since the time of Galileo, the reasons for believing that the earth was round became successively more numerous. And yet it was only in the 1920's that a pilot of the American Air Corps photographed a section of the surface of the earth from a sufficient height to show the curvature of the earth. This photograph became a fact of observation. Before that, no matter how worthy were the reasons, the roundness of the earth was not a fact of observation. One could call it rather a fact of deduction.

So, in my opinion, the "fact" of evolution is a fact of deduction. Biological evolution seems a valid theory concerning the origin of successive plants and animals and of modern plants and animals. And it is the only positive theory on the scientific level.

Under this general heading of the theory of evolution would come a theory about a specific mechanism of evolution. Until a short time ago, what has been called the "synthetic theory" of evolution was the very best that one could achieve as a scientist (new evidence allows scientists to change and improve certain details). This theory unites all that has been learned about paleontology (the science of extinct animals and man), genetics (the science of heredity), and several special studies of living matter, such as those of populations, the relationships of organisms with their environment, the ancient geography of living beings, and other studies, particularly the experimental. A fine example of the experimental would be the work of Muller, who won a Nobel prize for discovering that irradiation of fruit flies with x-rays produced more than the normal number of mutations. Mathematics, too, has added considerably to man's knowledge.

But there is no such thing as the "last word" in science. One occasionally hears it said that there is no finality in science. Against a background of scholastic philosophy, one could not deny that there was finality in life; against the background of scholastic philosophy finality would mean a direction towards a final cause, which ultimately would be God. But what the scientist would mean is that there is no last word in science. Science can never say this is it, and it will never be different. Science attempts continually to make a better link between its ideas and reality. Hypotheses and theories at any given time are the best link between the two. So, the synthetic theory is finding that new developments are budding from it.

However the situation may be with regard to the mechanics of evolution, everyone will admit that the evidence for the "fact" of evolution is extremely strong. It is true that a source of confusion for the layman may lie in the use of the word "evolution" for different processes in various science: physics, biology, social science. We cannot discuss these differences here. But we can say that evolution, in the very general sense of the word, has become a dimension of modern thought.

The topic, "Evolution and Philosophy," is not particularly helpful because we are not only going to deal with pure reason (with which philosophy is concerned), but with reason as used by man. Man does not exist in a purely philosophical realm; he exists here and now, and he is greatly influenced by his fellow men. As the anthropologist would put it, he exists in a *culture*. The word "culture" is shorthand for the total complex of the group ways of doing things at any given point in time and in a specific space.

We must face the fact that we have to deal with people—theoretical-minded people and practical people, and every other kind of people—who live in a concrete existence. Nevertheless, in this small section of our discussion we will try to start out with some concepts of pure reason.

One of the excrescences on the theory of evolution appeared very early, after the initial shock of Darwin, and this excrescence is materialism. Materialism states very simply that there is nothing else than matter in the world: there is no spirit, no soul in man, and of course, no God. Darwin himself made no pronouncements on this matter, but his first English apostle, Thomas Huxley, although he called himself an agnostic, in practice preached materialism. So did another great early apostle of Darwinism, in Germany, Ernst Haeckel. And they had many followers.

Another difficulty about the writings of some evolutionists who do not realize that they have invaded the field of philosophy is the denial of purpose in the biological universe. This involves two overlapping but essentially separate ideas. One may be summed up under the scholastic word "finalism." Their denial of finalism would mean that there was no end, in a sense of a goal, for these biological entities. This in its turn involves a denial of God, who is the Goal of everything outside of Himself. It also involves an ignoring of any possibility that God has inserted into evolution any goal at all.

Essentially, the scientific facts of evolution do not form any reasonable and immediate basis for a philosophy of progress. The Christian philosophy of life, however, does include this concept when it proposes the concept of Divine Providence. It is commonly thought that evolution and the idea of progress are intimately related. This is not true. By common consent in our time, any such "value judgment" as the idea of progress is excluded from the scientific realm. Also excluded is any idea that beings possess an internal principle which would make them work toward a definite end. For the scientist, precisely as a scientist, it is true that these concepts are unprovable. But for the complete human being, who is also a philosopher and to a certain extent a theologian, this is not the case.

Harking back to the distinction of levels—the scientific, the philosophical, the theological—perhaps we may introduce a short quotation from a non-Catholic scientist, one who appreciates the total facts of life. "Man lives in two worlds (or perhaps more) . . . there is a field, or world, of science in which questions posed in scientific terms get scientific answers; and another world where words like belief, love, splendor and majesty have meaning. This other world refuses to be shut out of our experience" (C. A. Coulson, *Science and Christian Belief*).

One of the most loudly proclaimed conclusions of those scientists of the synthetic school who have written in the philosophical vein is the fact that chance has ruled out God, Divine Providence, and finalism. Such scientists do not realize that what may seem chance to them is not necessarily chance to God. God is so much greater than our minds can define that we may safely allow not only that he foresaw all the results of the mechanism which He set in motion in creating the universe, but also that He could use "chance" precisely as a mechanism of His universe!

George Gaylord Simpson denies finalism on the basis of a finding like the following. Remarking on what has been the showcase evidence for evolution—namely, the development of the modern horse—he makes the point that the older evolutionary schemes showed a direct, straight line of descent from the earliest four-toed horse to the modern one-toed horse. However, says he, what actually happened at any given point in time was like fireworks. All sorts of forms developed and showered out around the one form which then moved on to the next one. Inasmuch as the forms which were not ancestral to the next development were useless, they became extinct. This is a famous example of "chance."

I certainly do not see how one must demand of God that our evolutionary picture be one of straight lines from form to form, without any "wastage." Do we know that these extinct forms did not fulfill a certain function in their time?

It would be interesting to describe the effect of Darwinism and, more importantly, the works of Herbert Spencer, the earliest modern philosopher of evolution, on American business, politics, and general culture. But there is not room for that discussion in this chapter. The most amazing conclusions were drawn. "The survival of the fittest" was used by American courts to frustrate any forward-looking legislation with regard to the common man, labor, and the well-known private enterprise system.

To give merely one brief example from this period, John D. Rockefeller told a catechism class of the Baptist Church that the American private enterprise system was like the American Beauty Rose. It derived its beauty from the fact that all the other buds on the stem were pinched off. This demonstrated, said he, the fact that the survival of the fittest was "a law of Nature and of Nature's God."

Today we are aware that one can derive no valid ethics from the scientific theory of evolution, no matter how this may be expressed. Man is greater than the scientific realm, greater than evolution, and the sources of his total nature are to be found in more than these sources.

Catholic theologians, too, do not accept materialism, the denial of finalism, or, in a realm which bridges the gap between philosophy and theology, the denial of Divine Providence.

At the time of the appearance of Darwin's *Origin*, theologians had to deal with a situation which involved not only this new theory of biological evolution but also vicious attacks on the truthfulness of the Bible. These theologians, too, had to take into account the political, economic and literary scene. Although they were not scientists, they had to ask the scientist about the facts in the case. It is hardly ever mentioned in the history of evolution that the evidence for the evolution of man at the time of Darwin's *Origin* was nonexistent. Indeed, for many years following 1859, the evidence, to the theologian who asked the scientist what was going on, seemed extremely contradictory.

In dealing with the theological attitude about human evolution, we will sketch briefly the period from 1859 to the present.

On the Origin of Species by Darwin proclaimed to the Western world an idea new to everyone, theologians included. In general, the first reviews of this book by Catholics were not favorable. However, some Catholics such as St. George Mivart, a prominent British biologist, thought highly of evolution if not of Darwinism. (Darwinism, strictly speaking, implies a very specific mechanism for evolution; its use to indicate evolution as a whole is natural, but confusing.) Mivart was given an honorary degree by the pope for his book on evolution.

Shortly thereafter a reaction set in, as it became clear that the concept of evolution could be dangerous. It was dangerous not in itself, precisely (although weaknesses of proof and incompatibility with some traditional Catholic views were recognized), but because it joined forces with other ideas, such as materialism, which were inimical to the Catholic religion. For a number of years those Catholics who expressed approval of evolution in any way were quietly asked by the Roman officials to withdraw their books.

In 1906, the newly founded Biblical Commission issued a set of decrees concerning the interpretation of Sacred Scripture, and these decrees touched on the subject of evolution. The Biblical Commission followed the Catholic attitude and method by not leaning too strongly either in the direction of fundamentalism or in that of modernism. Fundamentalism would have us believe that every word of the Sacred Scriptures as it has come down to us at this particular moment is to be taken in its most naive "literal" sense. Modernism, on the other hand, would characterize most of the Old and the New Testaments as a set of beautiful myths, with religious intent and importance to be sure, but with no necessary relation to history or reality. The Biblical Commission indicated that there was indeed a history behind the words of Holy Writ but that these Scriptures were not written in the fashion of modern scientific history. The Biblical Commission certainly had to hold fast to certain basic facts of the Catholic Faith such as the creation of man, the fact of original sin, the fact of redemption, and the like. And to these it held fast.

A landmark in the development of the opinion of Catholic theologians about evolution occurred with the publication of a book by Canon Dorlodot (the English edition appeared in 1922) in which the author not only showed a favorable attitude toward evolution in general but laid the groundwork for the study of the fathers of the Church in this connection. Dorlodot was followed in 1932 (in *Evolution and Theology*) by his pupil, Father Messenger. Some parts of this book are no longer of particular value, but its study of the fathers of the Church is the best that has been done up to this time and shows that the fathers might have been more flexible in dealing with evolution than were most modern theologians.

Following these authors a number of clerics indicated their favorable attitude towards evolution, and none of them has been asked to withdraw his works. The negative argument here is rather strong. We well know that Rome knows exactly what is being taught and written throughout the Church; if it does not condemn a particular work or a particular trend of doctrine, then we feel rather safe in following it.

The latest official ecclesiastical document on this subject is contained in the encyclical of Pope Pius XII, *Humani generis*.

This encyclical tells us that the question of human evolution is a free one at this time, to be scientifically and fairly discussed by scientists both sacred and profane. It states that a Catholic has to believe in the spirituality of the human soul (a doctrine defined in the fourteenth century) and that a Catholic should be willing to consent to any future judgment of the Church in the matter of evolution. There is really no point in being a Catholic unless a man is so disposed.

The pope also notes that one should not treat evolution as if it were a proven fact, and indeed, in view of our knowledge that science can never utter the final word, this is not surprising. Finally, the pope rules out a doctrine called "Polygenism," which would teach that mankind sprang from a number of ancestors. We know from Revelation that all of present-day mankind descended from a single pair, Adam and Eve. About this pair science knows nothing, but Revelation teaches us that they existed; it does not tell us when or where. These points are not essential.

All theologians agree that God is the Creator of all things, including man. All theologians agree that God had to take a direct part in the creation of man, particularly because of the fact that he has a spiritual soul. No machinery of the material universe that God could have set up to bring about the evolution of any material body could eventuate in a spiritual soul. The material universe simply does not have this kind of power.

One thing is certain. Today, as in 1859, Catholic theologians are stating that any theory of evolution which allows for the human spirit is not against any Catholic dogma. In addition, there is a certain change of opinion among many Catholic theologians, which renders them much more favorable to a spiritualistic evolution.

This change has been brought about by one fact which is important, but which is outside of theology as such and by another fact which is interior to theology.

The scientific evidence for human evolution has increased immensely in the last few years. At the time of Darwin, it was practically nonexistent; today, it is very strong indeed. This has made an impression on theologians.

Secondly, there have been changes in the attitudes of students of Sacred Scripture. We do not have space enough to go into them at length here, but these changes amount to very different interpretations of certain portions of Sacred Scripture than we had even a few years ago. Scripture scholars have been examining the literary forms of Scripture with great profit, and, without falling into modernism, have been moving Catholic opinion farther from fundamentalism.

Let us propose one brief example. Some years ago, Catholic scholars told us that it must be taken literally that Eve was taken physically from the body of Adam. This opinion they no longer demand. Inspecting the literature as they have it before them, they would say that there is a spiritual lesson that God wanted to teach in this part of Genesis, but that we do not have to take it as a literal, physical fact that Eve came from the body of Adam. The lesson may well be that Eve is also human (this is a particularly necessary lesson in the Near East, where woman is not as highly regarded as she is among us). The lesson may well be that man is the head of the family. Certainly, the basic and absolute unity of mankind is an important concept in the consideration of human nature. Whatever the lesson may be, it is not necessary to believe literally in the physical derivation of the body of Eve from the body of Adam.

This is only one example, and it is regrettable that further examples cannot be given here, because perhaps some may wonder what one *does* have to believe from Sacred Scripture, in terms of modern interpretation. We have to believe exactly what we always had to believe, as the fundamental lessons of a religious book, which is what the Bible is. Thus there is no question now and there never has been any question that God is the Creator of all things. This is important. Exactly how it may have been expressed several thousand years ago for people in the Near East without our present-day outlook in things scientific and literary, is important only inasmuch as we understand the truths God taught then and now. And we can grow in our appreciation of the richness and grandeur of these teachings, and in their relationships with ongoing human life.

We might add a few words about evolution and Catholic life. It may seem strange to many that evolution can contribute to Catholic life and devotion.

Let us, for the moment, presume that evolution is a reality. Let us also postulate that the universe in which evolution occurs is God's. What are the consequences of these two points of departure?

One conclusion is certainly the fact that the material universe is important. It is important because God has created it. By this very fact alone the material universe is worthy of being the object of the consideration and the study of a Catholic. This means that chemistry, biology, physics, and people are objects of study which are worthy of the human intellect.

This means, too, that the universe has a sacramental nature. We of the urban world of today have practically forgotten this fact. Our "primitive ancestors" appreciated very well indeed, in their own way, this sacramental nature of the universe, because religion was woven in and throughout their whole world, all their actions and thoughts.

Granted that the material universe is important in itself, and is important sacramentally, we then find, theologically, that the universe is even more important. Why?

Because the universe has, in a manner of speaking, been assumed by the Second Person of the Blessed Trinity, when He assumed human nature. The dynamic view of the universe that evolution gives us shows that Christ did not assume a nature which was, so to speak, artificially and arbitrarily placed at the summit of the visible universe. He assumed a nature which had genetic relationships with the rest of this universe. Man was not simply placed in the primacy of the visible universe, he grew into it. The atoms, the molecules, the one-celled animals and plants, the many-celled animals, the reptiles, the mammals, all of these and everything in the universe are his cousins. They are more than his cousins, they are his ancestors.

Therefore, in assuming human nature, Christ in some sense assumed these too. And He assumed all the multiplicity and the vicissitudes of the universe and its history, as it shows itself not only in complexity but in the absolutely amazing unity of God's plan and creative reality. This plan we shall all really appreciate only on the day of the Last Judgment.

And more than this. Christ not only assumed the past of the universe, but He assumed its future. If there is a goal in evolution, it is God. And Christ not only became man but is and remains God.

By reinstituting a supernatural order, Christ made it possible that we should be and should be called the sons of God; this we had forfeited in Adam; this we regained in Christ. Christ did more than simply redeem us, He put the whole universe, through us, back in order. In the end He will gather up us, and the universe, both natural and supernatural, all virtues and all progress, all evolution unto the fulness of being according to the Divine Will.

Thus, in our meditations we can well consider our blood relationship with the whole of the material universe, and through Christ with the whole of the spiritual universe, with the whole of the past, and the whole of the future.

Social Change in the City Parish

REV. JOSEPH P. FITZPATRICK, S.J.*

IT DOES NOT require much reflection to make people aware that the Catholic parish in the city is in the midst of unprecedented change. The main lines of change are obvious and are in two directions: the upheaval of the parish in the center of the older city where former residents are moving out by the thousands, and new and strange residents are moving in by the hundred thousands; and secondly, the rise of the new parish in the suburbs. These are not two different things, but two aspects of the same thing, namely: the shifting pattern of city life in its adjustment to new residents, new technologies, new means of transportation and new values. These two main lines of physical change are the reflection in the visible order of a much more subtle but

* Father Fitzpatrick is associate professor of sociology and industrial relations at Fordham University, past president of the *American Catholic Sociological Society*, lecturer at Area Studies Institute, Catholic University of Puerto Rico, and author of articles which have appeared in leading journals.

much more important change: the move from lower to higher social and economic status.

These changes have been upsetting. The pastor sees his older parish become a colored parish in less than twenty years; a family decides to move away from the invading Puerto Ricans; the owner of a pleasant home finds a low-cost housing project built across the street; the newlyweds head for the suburbs only to find the economic pressures almost too great to bear; these are but a few of the facets of the complicated changes of modern life. They are the price we pay for the city; and many raise the lament that the price is too high.

This article aims to put these changes in perspective by relating them to the impact they have on the city parish.

It is common for a city parish in the United States to witness more change in ten years than many a rural parish in Europe would have witnessed in ten centuries. The basic design of parish living in the past developed around the stable rural parish with the stable rural community. The parish now finds itself confronted with changes so rapid they are bewildering. The great challenge in our day, therefore, is the adjustment of parish life to these rapid changes so that the parish may be as vital and meaningful a thing to the city dweller as it was to the rural parishioner a century ago.

In order to draw the perspective, we shall try to explain three things: 1) The specialization of life in the modern city, or what could be called the loss of functions in the city parish; 2) the mobility of people;

3) the loss of a sense of community, or a sense of belonging, and the means by which this may be restored.

Specialization of Life

It is not by chance that the city has become the dominant factor in modern life. In 1950, 64 per cent of all people in the United States lived in cities. When the 1960 census data are published, they will indicate that over 70 per cent of all Americans today live in cities. Not only is the city the place where most Americans live, but they live rather densely in them. The nighttime population of Manhattan Island is 80,000 per square mile; the workday population of Radio City alone is equal to half the total population of the state of Nevada.

The reason why this kind of concentration is possible and necessary is the fact that the American way of life has become a highly technical thing, supported by a vast array of specializations. This is the result of modern science. If the 55,000 people who work every day in Radio City were herding sheep, they would need the whole of Manhattan Island for each to have a patch of grass for his flock; if they were farmers, they would need more than Manhattan Island to enable them to grow enough food to survive. But specialization has mechanized the farm and released millions for other tasks, and they have been absorbed in thousands of other specializations from the typing of letters to the selling of wheat and the keeping of accounts. They use the money they get from their specialization to purchase the food that specialized farmers grow for them, that specialized truckmen bring to them and specialized merchants sell to them in a supermarket.

Specialization has brought great benefits to modern life, but it has also made men extremely dependent one upon the other. It has placed in the hands of specialists the many functions which support life. The specialists by and large do their work well; but they have left us helpless and dependent in almost every aspect of our existence. The child is born in the hospital under the care of expert specialists; if a man gets sick, he is treated in a hospital; education takes place largely outside the home and is provided by specialists; the car is serviced by specialists, runs on gas that is produced by specialists, travels on highways that are built by specialists and carries people to the office where they do their own specialized work.

The point of these remarks is obvious. A man can live in a city because thousands of people are available to provide the specialized service he needs in order to live; and a man must live in a city because only there can the services be made available. Only there can he himself generally find a service to perform in order to earn his own living.

It would require a book to review all the effects of these changes on human life. We propose to examine how they affect the parish. The parish at one time was the vital center of a self-sustaining and vigorous life. The strength and solidarity of the parish reflected the strength and solidarity of a community where people were self-reliant, knew each other, helped each other, worked with each other. It was once the center of a complete and full human life. Its close relationship to these vital functions made the parish strong.

With increasing specialization, the parish has now become largely a place where people come home to sleep. They work outside the parish; after parochial school, they go outside the parish for education. Recreation is largely professional and is brought from outside the parish into the parlor through TV. As a result, the parish also has become a specialized center where experts provide religious care and spiritual services, while the larger segments of the lives of parishioners work themselves out elsewhere, far removed from the influence and even the knowledge of the parish leaders.

The family has lost its functions to the specialist and the neighborhood and parish have lost their functions with it. This is the price Americans have paid for that scientific progress which has given us so many benefits. But one result of this progress is the large and complicated city which is the center of many of the problems that are caused by constant change.

Mobility

When they think of the problems of the city, most people think of them in terms of the movement of people—particularly the invasion of Negroes and Puerto Ricans and the consequent departure of older citizens. The situation is often described as a sad one in which new and "undesirable" elements drive out the older and more "desirable" ones. The city, as a result, faces the problem of slums, deterioration, and slow but certain death.

It is helpful to see the problem of the movement of people in its relationship to the city. The growth of the city is the central social phenomenon of our time. This is happening all throughout the world. In the United States alone, between 1930 and 1950, more than sixteen million people moved from farms to the city; they have continued to move with the result that only 10 per cent of the population of the United States now live on farms. Between 1820 and 1930, more than forty million people came from Europe to the United States, most of them to the growing American cities. More than 5 per cent of the population of the United States move their residence across county lines every year. This involved a total of seven and a half million people last year. The present movement of Negroes and Puerto Ricans to New York is simply one aspect of a massive movement of people that has been taking place in the United States for over a century.

Why all this movement? It is partly the movement of people following job opportunities, whether they are managers moved by their company or displaced workers seeking jobs. Partly it is the response of unskilled people to the demand for cheap labor in the cities. It is partly people in poorer areas seeking an opportunity of something better in the city. Whatever the reason, it is a universal phenomenon of great proportions and it is directly related to the city.

This migration of people has always been attended by distress, sometimes greater, sometimes less. It places a great burden on established residents. It creates complicated problems for the new migrants. It is possible for the inrush of migrants to overwhelm a city. But New York, for the most part, has profited from its newcomers in the past. There is every reason to believe that it will profit from its newcomers now.

In 1950 there were 750,000 Negroes in New York. By 1960 there were more than a million. In 1950 there were 250,000 Puerto Ricans in the City. In 1960, it is reported there are 612,000. Actually, in the perspective of migrations, this still does not equal the great migrations of the past; but it is a formidable number of newcomers who must become adjusted to the city's life.

It is in terms of smaller units, however, that one begins to see the impact of the movement on parish life. Let us take as an example a parish on the lower East side, which was established over a century ago as an Irish parish; in 1917 it was turned over to the Jesuit Fathers to be conducted as an Italian parish; it is now rapidly becoming a Puerto Rican parish. In April, 1954, a census was taken there. The census recorded three thousand Puerto Ricans living in the parish. In November another census was taken in the same parish; this census recorded five thousand Puerto Ricans, an increase of two thousand in seven months. A special study of one block of the parish indicated that in April twenty-six Puerto Rican families were located on the block. In November there were still twenty-six Puerto Rican families on the block but twenty-one were different families. This represented a turnover of about 80 per cent in seven months.

A second example is found in the experience of the largest parish in the area of the new Lincoln Square development. In 1947, three thousand people were displaced from the parish to make room for a low cost housing project; in 1949, one thousand new families moved into the project. In 1953, just across from the church in the area behind the New York Coliseum, three hundred and fifty dwelling units were demolished to make room for the high rental apartments that are now there. The Lincoln Square redevelopment began about 1958 and relocated more than five thousand families in two years, most of them from this same parish. This is the intensity of change that can strike a parish in a city like New York.

This kind of change has led to two important phenomena: it has created in the center of the city what is called the "missionary" parish and has created in the suburbs the rapidly growing number of new parishes, with young, vigorous, often well-educated Catholic people who show promise of developing a particularly dynamic Catholic life.

It is the city parish, the missionary parish, to which I would like to direct my attention. The migration has brought into the older parishes either large numbers of Puerto Ricans—most of them nominally Catholic and poorly instructed in their Faith, all of them unfamiliar with the kind of Catholic life they meet in the New York City parish—or large numbers of Negroes, most of them Protestant, most of them with deep religious feelings but with little instruction in religion, who participate actively in no Church at all.

Many of the older residents greet these rapid changes by running away. It is very doubtful that this is the wisest way to meet the challenge. His Eminence, Cardinal Spellman, and the parishes of his Archdiocese, however, are making an extraordinary effort to meet this challenge. His Eminence has long since decided to provide spiritual care for the Puerto Ricans, not by setting up separate parishes for Puerto Ricans, but by making every effort to integrate them into existing parishes where, geographically, they are located in large numbers. As a result, there are now more than one hundred parishes in the New York Archdiocese that provide special care and services for Spanish speaking people. More than two hundred priests of the archdiocese have been trained in the use of the Spanish language. This represents an apostolate that is little less than phenomenal. It seems at present to be hopelessly inadequate, but it will bear abundant fruit in the years to come.

The crucial role in the integrated parish must be played not so much by priests as by lay people. The parish is faced with a situation of thousands of Puerto Ricans coming from a homeland where the way of life is very different from our own, and where the practice of the Faith is very different also. It is important that they be received by Catholics who respect them, accept them, understand the background from which they come and their different way of life. If they are not accepted with kindness and respect, it is doubtful that they will ever become interested in parish life. In this way, thousands could be lost to the Faith. The priests who are working among the Puerto Ricans always insist that their greatest help, or greatest obstacle, is the attitude of the lay people of the parish, because the lay people are the ones who sit beside the newcomer in the subway or meet him in the supermarket, the barbershop or the corner bar. They are the ones who meet the newcomer at work, play beside him in the park, wait with him to get into the same movie house. It is in these situations where "acceptance" is so critical that the stranger comes to feel he is or is not wanted, that he is or is not respected as "one of our own" in Christ.

The Negro situation is much more complicated, and much more difficult. The real problem here is not that of persuading white parishioners not to leave when Negro people begin to move in. The problem is in the suburbs to which the white parishioners have fled. Generally, these become social bastions raised against the influx of a single colored person. In this way, what appears to be the center of a dynamically developing Catholic life, may, in the long run, become a colossal failure of charity and justice.

The Negro must be brought into effective contact with the Catholic Church, which means he must be brought into effective contact with Catholic people, the vast majority of whom are white. It does not appear possible for this effective contact to be achieved outside of a neighborhood situation. The segregation that results automatically from the pattern of suburban living may isolate the Catholic completely from that contact with the Negro which is necessary to bring the Negro to the Faith. The suburban Catholic thus may be devoting himself to the cultivation of a vigorous Catholic life in a situation which prevents him from facing the central challenge to Catholic life today.

Briefly, these are the difficulties which rapid mobility creates for the city parish at the present time.

The Loss of Community

Both factors—the great specialization of modern life and the great movement of people in modern cities —have led to the loss of what is called "community," that is: those close relationships of people to each other which give men a sense of satisfaction, of having the support of relatives and friends, of being recognized and respected for what one is and for what he does for the people among whom he lives. The parish has ceased to be what it so clearly was in the past: a community. The old loyalties, the old solidarity of the immigrant neighborhoods, of the villages and towns, have disintegrated. Thus far, it is doubtful whether any other loyalties and solidarities have taken their place.

This defines the problem of the modern parish. Can there be an active and vigorous Catholic life if parish life has become simply one small segment of a person's existence? In former times, such things as the blessing of the fields at sowing time, the ceremonies at harvest time, the blend of religious devotion and recreation in the celebration of religious festivals, the rhythm of life from birth and baptism to marriage to death, all provided a situation in which faith and religious devotion penetrated every aspect of a parishioner's life. Life was "integrated." There was a wholeness to it, a consistency, a meaning that was ever present, that made it rich and kept the parish at the heart of man's existence. Now, however, when the Mount Carmel Procession passes through the streets of an Italian neighborhood, the old folks are walking in it, but many of the middle aged are sitting before the TV. Many of the youngsters are at the ball game or the neighborhood dance. This is not said in criticism, but as a clear indication that the old solidarities are gone. How does the Church give a meaningful blessing to the work of her children in the parish when the list of occupations would cover five or six pages of an occupation manual? With people shifting around as they are shifting today, how can solidarities be built? Does this mean that the parish must cease to be a significant factor in the lives of people? What is its place in the modern city?

The problem of community is illustrated by the success of store-front Churches among the Puerto Ricans in New York. In a study of ten Catholic parishes in the Bronx last year we located eighty-seven store-front Churches in the geographical area of the ten Catholic parishes. These churches had a combined membership of well over five thousand people. The participation of these Puerto Ricans in the Pentecostal and Evangelical Sects which operate in the store-fronts appears to us to be a serious and sincere religious experience. In attempting to explain the attraction of the sects for people traditionally Catholic, we are impressed by the strong sense of belonging which these people find in the storefronts, the satisfaction they seem to derive from participating actively in the services with people of their own kind, and in an atmosphere where they feel, as they expressed it, "at home." The store-front churches attract the Puerto Ricans because, in the bewilderment of a large city, they provide a sense of community. The Catholic Church would be more attractive to the Puerto Ricans if some of these characteristics of "being among their own," of "being at home," of being accepted by a strong supporting group, could become part of the Catholic parish. Puerto Ricans will be more responsive to the parish if it can succeed in being more of a "community" to them.

The achievement of this kind of community will require an extraordinary creative effort in the modern city. The renewed emphasis on the liturgy and on active participation in the life of the Church are indications of this striving for community. Efforts such as the Christian Family Movement, the Young Christian Workers and so many others are further efforts to recreate solidarity on the basis of our Faith.

Therefore, the picture is not one entirely of distress. It has elements of real hope. The situation does not indicate that a strong parish life cannot be created; it may mean that it cannot be created on the basis of the same social factors that supported it previously. It will have to be created out of a firm commitment of Catholics to the clear values of Catholic life.

In the past, the loyalties of a traditional Catholic parish were not entirely loyalties to the Faith. They were loyalties of isolated rural family groups in which the kinship tie was often the really binding element that provided strength to the Faith. They were loyalties of underprivileged ethnic groups clinging together for protection and help in the midst of large cities. Devotion to the faith and the parish was, as often as not, only a symbol of loyalty to the ethnic or nationality group. They were loyalties of class groups, either higher class or lower class; in the United States most commonly they were lower class. It was the sense of solidarity with the class group that gave men a sense of solidarity in their Faith. Now all this has changed. The parish is no longer one of a common life; people are highly diversified in their special callings and occupations. It is no longer an Irish parish or an Italian or a German parish. It is a mixture of a dozen or more nationality groups who speak strange tongues and live according to strange ways. Thus we approach the period when the unity of the parish will have to be really a "religious" unity; a unity in "faith," because there are so few other unities that can bind the people together. This will lead to a unity in the spirit, rather than a unity of blood, or racial background, or economic interest, or class position. This, if it occurs, will lead to a strengthening of parish life and of Catholic responsibilities.

In summary, therefore, what is taking place is an effort to bring the life of the parish into a meaningful relationship to the specialized life and the rapid mobility and change which are part of the kind of society we live in. If Catholics can succeed in doing this, not only will life in the city be elevated and inspired, but the life of the Church in the parish will be made more dynamic and rich by its contact with the human experience of the modern city.

Theological Problems in Mass Communications

Very Rev. Msgr. Timothy J. Flynn*

T̶HE STORY of the twentieth century could be called the story of mass communications—the story of a complex network of industries sufficiently dominant in our culture to raise theological questions. But before considering what theological problems might be involved in modern mass communications, it might be well to consider the highly developed, extensive, and sophisticated nature of communications in present-day society. Weekly, millions of words, concrete images, abstract concepts, new and often appealing values bombard the human ear, eye, and imagination through a variety of print and electronic media. Any attempt to comprehend the sheer size and complexity of mass communications in contemporary society staggers the mind.

* Monsignor Flynn is director of radio and television and of the Bureau of Information, Archdiocese of New York. He is consultor to the Secretariat on Mass Communications of Vatican Council II.

For example, the wires of the Associated Press teletype into the newsrooms of newspapers across the country an estimated one and one quarter million words per day. Its radio wire distributes to radio newsrooms sixty words per minute over a twenty-four-hour period. This is just one wire service; there are others.

In New York City alone there are a total of twenty-nine daily newspapers, English and foreign language, not to mention the weeklies and bi-weeklies—both regional and neighborhood—all of which have their own readers. They carry not merely straight news but comments as well; the editorials, the columnists, the glamorized features. They are journals of opinion as well as vehicles of information.

The field of motion pictures is a communications medium with characteristics all its own. From April 1, 1959, to March 31, 1960, the motion picture department of the New York State Education Department licensed for exhibition in New York seven hundred and ninety-nine feature films, both Hollywood product and imports, all of which were exhibited in the almost clinically perfect atmosphere of a darkened theatre where attention is focused on a single bright area on which the message unfolds without either distraction or interruption.

More than three thousand radio stations operate at present in the United States, many of them approaching twenty-four-hour-a-day service. This communications industry has grown and has not dwindled since the advent of television. It is not merely the size of radio that is staggering, but its omnipresence. It takes ingenuity and energy to escape a medium whose receivers are in bedrooms and kitchens. Moreover, sales of car radios have tripled in ten years, so that now over 83 per cent of the new cars purchased are radio equipped; portable sets almost drown the sound of wind and waves at the seashore, and transistor portables fit conveniently into one's shirt pocket.

The all-pervading presence of electronic communications is apparent also in the case of television. Ninety per cent, or a total of 49,000,000 of American homes are equipped with television, and almost seven million of those homes have more than one television set. There are 541 commercial television stations in 332 cities. The seven stations in New York City alone telecast approximately 800 hours of programming a week—more, in fact, than the annual output of Hollywood.

Moreover, television is a medium that attracts audiences of almost unbelievable size. In 1959 the popular weekly program *Gunsmoke* attracted 41,000,000 viewers and retained this number over a period of six months. The ten most popular television programs have averaged thirty-two million viewers each. Into this communications medium the one hundred top advertisers in the nation have poured $1,700,000,000 for advertising purposes in a single year—an indication of their evaluation of its audience and its impact.

And have developments stopped? Literally on our horizons there looms today the prospect of earth satellites designed to make communications more world-wide and more instantaneous than it is now. Developments are limited only by scientific ingenuity and human resources.

In view of all that is now in operation—and there are other communications media we have not mentioned —the present generation is the best, or at least the most informed generation in history. But we are also the most besieged mentally; we are subjected by advertisers to calculated stimuli; our motivations are researched; our reactions tabulated. Directives to make more efficient the assault on the human will are outlined by Edward L. Bernays (*Engineering of Popular Consent*) and deplored by Vance Packard (*Hidden Persuaders*).

The field has become an area for informed Catholic writing. Dr. Rodolfo Arata, director of Radio-Televisione Italiana and author of *Fundamentals of Esthetic Judgment,* has stated: "The great conquests of science and technology impose upon us the necessity of a constant deepening of spiritual values and a strengthening of the moral conscience since, otherwise, what should be a source of human progress can become the instrument of apocalyptical destruction." Father William Lynch, S.J., in his perceptive study of *The Image Industries* has outlined a theological concern about modern communications. In his analysis, the image industries, in the hands of a few (the controlling commercial interests) have imposed upon men through the manipulation of the national imagination a uniform mass culture that is disruptive of the very shape of the human soul. These manipulators of the image industries so blanket our senses, focus our imagination, channel our attention and exclude wider considerations that the rational soul is held captive and its volitions guided. "The responsibility of our mass media . . . is so great that it is almost incalculable, so powerful is their control over our most intimate and everyday images and, therefore, over our final attitudes and decisions." This is surely a theological problem and the creative religious mind must bring its influence to bear upon it.

In an age whose single most prominent characteristic is its power of rapid communication, it is not surprising to see the Church turn its attention to the vast and influential media of press, radio and television, communications media that work upon the human mind, influence attitudes, fill imaginations with images and attempt to bear in some way upon the human will. The Church has no choice but to come to grips with such an influence and try to develop a salutary approach toward it.

Everyone from the press agent to the statesman has utilized mass communications to achieve his own particular end. Advertisers use the "hard sell" and the "soft sell." Nor are all the uses good. Our generation has been dominated by propaganda and nations have been subverted by the "Big Lie." Truth faces a struggle in the world. But the Church's attention to mass communications is not solely negative, critical or censorious.

The Church has been immersed in the field of communications ever since the day when Christ gave to His apostles the mandate "go, teach all nations." She has been the great communicator since her inception. When Peter preached, when the evangelists wrote, when medieval monks in their *scriptoria* copied manuscripts and built libraries, when missionaries traveled and bishops, as an extension of their teaching office, founded schools and colleges, they were communicating as God has intended them to do—with the effective means and methods that their respective ages made available to them. We have witnessed the rapid advance of communications in the last few decades and we find in the last few years a particular interest manifested by the Church in this area of communications. It is an area which presents to the Church both promise and problems, opportunities and obstacles.

In September of 1957, Pope Pius XII issued an encyclical *Miranda Prorsus* which dealt with motion pictures, radio, and television and which was hailed in Catholic circles as a type of Magna Charta for these industries. In February of 1959, Pope John XXIII issued a *motu proprio Boni Pastoris* establishing the Pontifical Commission for Motion Pictures, Radio, and Television as a permanent office of the Holy See attached to the Vatican Secretariate of State. He referred then to motion pictures, radio, and television as "among these factors of modern civilization which influence the spiritual life of man." There have been many statements by Vatican officials encouraging the use of these media for apostolic purposes. With the announcement in 1960 of the formation of the preparatory commission for the coming second Vatican Council, a secretariate was established to deal with the mass media, not to facilitate the reporting of events of the coming Council, but rather to draw up recommendations regarding the mass media to be included, if deemed wise, in the agenda of the Council.

The attitude of the Church toward mass media has always been twofold: to utilize and to supervise—to use the public media as instruments of instruction to communicate effectively the message of the Gospel, to intensify the Christian life of the faithful, and to provide safeguards against the dangers to faith and morals. What we have noted about communications in the modern world would indicate that this twofold approach remains valid.

The activity of the Church in the field of mass media is also undergoing notable development. The Church could no more ignore the techniques of communication in the twentieth century than it could ignore the building of monastic libraries in the tenth, although we would like to see manifested now some of that zeal and creativity that went into the monastic *scriptoria.*

While the Church Universal is coping with the influence of communication in modern society and struggling to develop an application in modern times of the immutable age-old faith, the Church in our country has gone along in a pragmatic way responding to the urgent needs of each moment and has developed a large though not necessarily coordinated activity in this field.

In 1934, the National Legion of Decency was organized in the field of motion pictures. It operates in the second of the two interests of the Church, the field of moral supervision, with its classification of films according to their moral evaluation.

Within the past ten or more years approximately seventy dioceses in the United States have established bureaus of information to deal with the press, to make articulate to the press the life of the Church, bring its activities to public notice, obtain clarification on Church attitudes and teachings, and to do that required research for the general press which assures a more accurate portrayal of the Church to the public.

In approximately that same length of time some fifty dioceses have established offices for radio and television. A diocesan director of radio and television is a point of contact, a liaison between the broadcasting industry and the diocese for those religious matters with which broadcasters are concerned. He will interpret to them the mind of the Church. Not infrequently he will have to interpret to churchmen and to religious organizations within his diocese the peculiar needs, responsibilities, limitations and difficulties of the broadcasting industry. He will at times be invited to predict Catholic audience reaction to specific program situations or to act as a technical consultant so as to avoid portrayals of the Church that are not truly representative; and he will produce religious programs.

Of all the mass communications media, television is unique in one respect. It has, at least in the United States, a built-in concept of public service. In consequence there are a large number of Catholic programs of varying formats produced weekly throughout the breadth of the nation. In fact, this medium alone offers us an audience we can reach in no other way. A Trendex survey of Catholic television programs conducted in 1957 disclosed that 66 per cent of the audience is composed of non-Catholics. These are people to whom the teachings, life and attitudes of the Church must be communicated but who are not reached by the Catholic press—as extensive and diversified as it is—and certainly not by our schools or our preaching. This medium guarantees Catholics an opportunity to communicate with someone other than Catholics. In itself, the use of television, whether it be the production of the *ex-professo* Catholic religious program or the Catholic participation, lay and clerical, in general discussion programs dealing with areas of basically moral or doctrinal concern, constitutes one of the newest and most potent apostolates of modern times.

When we examine television from the moral standpoint, we realize that the Christianization of the medium is something which perhaps cannot be fully accomplished in our unconverted society. Mass communications in general, despite their power to mold and influence, cater to the most common taste, reflect society more than create it, follow social trends as much as lead them. What we find is the de-Christianized society of our day reflected, and its de-Christianization intensified and perpetuated. It is a mirror held up to our mores, with the viewer transfixed by the sight: a strange and mortal social vanity.

Edward R. Murrow thinks it is even less, that it is filled with vacuity and banality. It fails in its role as an instructor of the public. "Surely we must pay for using the most powerful instrument of communications to insulate the citizenry from the hard and dangerous realities which must be faced if we are to survive." He would be happy, he says, if it were only a mirror, even if it did no more than reflect our bigotries and intolerances.

It is, in large measure, for the average viewer, an escape, a flight into unreality. Television has competed with Hollywood only economically; in the field of entertainment it is a child of Hollywood in content and philosophy. With the exception of public service programming—religion, discussion of public issues, etc.— it offers much the same artistic fare as does Hollywood.

Toll TV, greatly heralded as an antidote to this state of affairs, probably would not create a demand for ballet and chamber music. It is visionary to think it would serve as a pedagogue, always leading the public to higher and higher planes. Once there is a box office, the appeal is to the masses. A box office exists now through the advertiser and we pay our toll for programming on the consumer products we buy. Toll TV is only a question of where you want the admission charge to be collected—the mass audience will be the same and will reflect the unchanged popular taste.

Yet, despite the realities we have observed, the influence of the Church should be on the side of the angels. We must always seek to elevate, to improve, to ennoble, to Christianize our environment, or we are renegade to our vocation in society.

It seems rash to speculate about the consequences of something that has not yet been initiated, but if Toll TV should join forces with the motion picture interests, as now seems likely, the work of the Legion of Decency will be rendered more difficult. The Hollywood product delivered effortlessly to the comfort of the home will eliminate, even more than TV has already done, more and more of the neighborhood theaters. The psychological impediment of publicly buying a ticket to a disapproved film will be removed. The exigencies of the medium will reduce the possibility of previewing, morally evaluating and forewarning the public. Hollywood and TV would be wed, and the former would then take on much of the instantaneous quality of the latter. Visionary? Perhaps, but what other trend or direction do we observe in this field?

At present television's moral excesses are not notable. The detectable damage done by TV is not occasioned by the rather rare program that offends seriously in morals, but rather by the constant exposure to the vapid, run-of-the-mill offerings that are being telecast on a round-the-clock basis from coast to coast. It is a damage to our intellect and also to our moral consciousness to be thus over exposed, by reason of the constant repetition of mundane standards and purely worldly and meretricious goals. The volume of output is so great it has to be in large part of little or no worth. In fact, there seems to be a careful cultivation of mediocrity in much of the fare. It is an industry that manifests a perverse power of reducing everything to a cliché.

In TV there is a problem of the admixture of show business (entertainment) with communications (education). This is present in the religious program. To convey your message you must hold your audience, and a certain professional competence in an unfamiliar area is required. Piety and good intentions will not compensate for a lack of professional competence. But at the hands of the industry, Church interests are sometimes made to suffer from an excess of emphasis on the show business end of broadcasting. The fifteen-minute (or thirty-minute) panel program with four guests, a moderator and two commercials, called together to discuss birth control, population problems, divorce laws, etc., is hardly intelligently exploring a subject. The laurels of victory, for which all panelists—and sometimes also the moderator—strive, go not to the balanced, informed, and responsible discussant, but rather to the coiner of the *mot juste*, to the dealer in the rapier thrust of wit. It becomes a contest of one-upmanship. To accept invitations to participate in programs of this sort is irresponsible. The subject matter has been chosen as a means of enticing an audience from a notoriously blasé public, not for the purpose of publicly elucidating a pressing issue of the day. TV's unsolved problem is whether the medium can mature. The "Play of the Week" at one time carried on some forty TV stations in the United States exposed a mass audience for the first time to the sophisticated content usually reserved to the Broadway stage or to the university drama department. The outcries have been loud; the critical acclaim high. In this case TV, with the innocence of youth, spoke with a frankness that Hollywood—always conscious of the mass audience—never would attempt. Contrast the "Play of the Week's" *Power and the Glory* with Hollywood's screen version *The Fugitive* starring Henry Fonda. The latter was more extensively and more definitely tailored to the limitations of a mass audience.

There is much to be said for caution here. TV has an audience unrestricted as to age, sex, intellectual maturity, economic status or anything else. There is also a difference in viewing habits. TV is viewed distractedly by an unforewarned audience, without the clinically perfect atmosphere of the theatre, where nuances can be observed and balancing factors can be presented.

It would seem that TV must exercise a greater restraint. Yet it admittedly cannot be limited to the level of the child viewer or to the mythical average twelve-year-old mentality of the public. A basic question of public service—the industry's obligation to broadcast in the public interest, convenience and necessity—is involved here. TV has not yet produced the creative genius to solve it.

In the area of moral protection the Church and the faithful have responded quickly to situations as they arose. The flood of paperback publications has been answered with the National Office for Decent Literature and its list of approved or disapproved reading for the young. Motion pictures, unheard of before the turn of the century, grew into a national moral problem by the 1920's, and the Legion of Decency was formed for moral guidance in the 1930's. But motion pictures as an industry, so large an element in popular entertainment a decade ago, is now undergoing radical change (neighborhood theaters have diminished somewhat and feature films are regularly seen on television in various cut and uncut versions), and television continues to find new forms and new adaptations. How communications will grow in the decade to come no one knows, other than that they will become more rapid, more inventive.

There is the possibility that moral listings in an age

of rapid communications will not always be effectively managed, that an attempt to establish such a listing will always find the Church agency with its feet dragging, its evaluations somewhat behind the distribution of the entertainment in question. The educated Catholic particularly should think through the problem that is inferred here.

Television as it now is does not lend itself to a listed moral evaluation of programs, principally because in this medium there is no opportunity to preview and to forewarn. Some less than adequate attempts have been made at program listings, such as the publication of feature films appearing on TV with their original Legion of Decency classifications, and lists of programs recommended on the basis of past performances.

It has been said that the demand for listings can at times indicate an intellectual stagnation, a recourse to Church agencies for specific directives in single instances rather than an exercise of the moral judgment that has been formed in the individual by years of Catholic education. It might also be regarded as a tribute to our American efficiency—or an indication of our organizational ability—that now, in the face of new communications media, we wish to see lists of the approved and disapproved programs multiplied.

It could, of course, be an unflattering reflection of our surrender to a push-button civilization that will provide instantaneous service and remove the necessity of individual moral judgment. But is it not rather a desperation move by people with moral sensitivity who cannot keep up with the flow of print and picture, electronic or otherwise, in their lives and in the lives of their children?

Meanwhile, until the suspected developments show signs of becoming actualized, the moral listings, as well as they can be managed, will serve as guides to a grateful public overwhelmed by the volume of sight and sound, images and concepts, values and emotional stimuli that bombard the consciousness of their harassed modern souls.

Catholicism and Mental Health

REV. GEORGE HAGMAIER, C.S.P.*

CATHOLICISM and mental health are two subjects which so dovetail, overlap, and influence each other that in this chapter we may give only the broadest examination to either subject.

"Mental health" is actually a misnomer. Those diseases or emotional disturbances usually listed under psychiatric abnormalities do not directly affect the mind, but the emotions. The mind—intellect and will—is not, generally speaking, sick. At times, intellect and will may be so overwhelmed by disordered feelings that they cannot function clearly, but this is a side effect of the emotional illness itself.

Until recently we had very little scientific knowledge about the emotions. The word "psychiatry" is only fifty years old. We must, however, hasten to add that

* Father Hagmaier is associate director of the Paulist Institute for Religious Research (New York) and instructor in pastoral psychology, Paulist House of Graduate Studies, Boston. He is co-author with Rev. Robert W. Gleason, S.J., of *Counselling the Catholic*.

some of the great writers, philosophers and spiritual guides of the past had important insights into the workings of the emotions. They wrote about them in an informal and intuitive fashion in terms of the general knowledge they had at the time.

Dynamic psychology has taught us many things which are new; at least things formerly known have been greatly elaborated upon in the light of recent discoveries. There is probably a great deal more that we do *not* know about mental health than what we do know about it. Much material in this field of psychiatry, psychology, and mental health is still hypothetical in character. We know that certain principles work in treating the mentally ill; we know a great number of techniques that will help them get well. We are not always sure, though, why they work. There is much study on many frontiers still to be done.

One of the reasons that the Catholic has a special difficulty with problems of mental health, emotions and behavior, is due to the heavy emphasis in our scholastic tradition on the intellect and the will as faculties which control behavior. Dynamic psychology, as we know, sees behavior as powerfully influenced by emotions and feelings. What is the truth here? Do intellect and will determine human behavior, or do emotions and feelings determine it? The problem for the Catholic is to reconcile this seeming conflict.

The Church quite rightly has designated a hierarchy of man's faculties. For example, she begins with the highest life of all, which is the supernatural life, the life of grace, of union with God, that life to which we have been raised and which is not a part of human nature as such. And then, in a secondary but very prominent position, the Church enthrones the intellect and the will. The ability to think, to arrive at judgments, and to make free choices are the highest natural faculties of man. Then, farther along the scale, the Church acknowledges the emotions and the passions as integral and essential to man's nature. The emotions and passions are "lower" in a sense, but inseparable from our humanity. In one sense, it is dangerous to speak of "higher" and "lower" because all of man's faculties belong to him. Together they make him a man. All are important.

The Church is quite right, however, in pointing out that the will and the intellect, enlightened and strengthened in the baptized person by grace, are supposed to control, to govern, to keep in check the more chaotic, emotional elements that are part of man. Hence for centuries the Church has used the catechism, the home, the pulpit, the confessional, to teach men an important truth: Train the intellect and will to keep the "lower" faculties, emotions and passions under control; learn to use them rightly.

Theologians generally affirm that the use of reason develops about the age of six or seven. It does not, of course, develop overnight. Its development is gradual.

The infant, the little baby, is a *feeling* creature long before it is a thinking or choosing creature. The emotions and the passions are there first and they are always at work. They are being influenced by outside people and things, and they are churning and stirring inside the little human being. What happens in those first five, six or seven years to the emotions and passions, to what one might call the active essence of this tiny human person, is most important.

There is truth in the dictum attributed to St. Ignatius: give me the child until he is seven and then you can do what you want with him. As the child grows toward that key age his personality congeals, in a sense, to a limited flexibility and the kind of character pattern he will have for life develops. A considerable degree of change is still possible, but the pathways by which future development takes place are fairly well determined. If one is an introvert at seven, he will likely be an introvert at seventy. One's adult fears and attitudes toward people, toward sexuality, toward authority, toward study, toward creativity are fairly well fixed by the age of seven. They are all rooted in the early feelings and experiences of the child.

A little baby is a bundle of feelings; he cries when he is hungry or wants to be changed; he is happy when he is cuddled and fed. His responses are essentially on an emotional level. It is only later that he integrates the thinking and the feeling elements in himself. And if this integration is muddled or blocked during the child's early years, he becomes confused, full of needless hostilities, anxieties, insecurities and fears. This is a serious state of affairs. We cannot repair a faulty set of emotions by means of the intellect alone. We cannot wipe away fears and anxieties as if man's personality were a slate that could be cleaned with a wet cloth.

Yet, this is what some people have tried to do. They

have supposed that they could treat mental illness without due regard for the emotions that cause it. Long before the time of Christ, the philosopher claimed that it was *his* task to cure the mentally ill, the emotionally disturbed. And some intellectuals still maintain that the trouble with a mentally sick person is that he does not think right—that when he *does* think right, he will be mentally healthy.

The legal profession also has long claimed jurisdiction over mental health because so much crime is due to mental sickness. And so, the lawyer or judge has said that the courts and penal institutions will punish and re-educate the criminally sick and return them to society, cured of their antisocial tendencies.

Interestingly enough, the medical profession also has been one of the greatest enemies of dynamic psychology. Many doctors have tended to regard all mental illness as an essentially organic thing, as an imbalance of chemistry or a lesion in the brain or the nervous system. While occasionally this is true, the psychoanalytic school and the dynamic psychologists believe that most mental illness is due to a malfunctioning of the emotions and that a long and careful examination of the patient's early years is required to determine how his emotions grew and became tangled, bitter, difficult to manage.

There are still those in the medical profession who seek to cure all mental illness with pills, electric shock and scalpel. While these means are helpful they often get at the symptoms only, not at the cause of the illness. The test, of course, comes when the patient is deprived of his tranquilizers. What happens when the effects of shock treatment wear off and certain patients experience the return of the symptoms whose cause lies in the deep recesses of the unconscious?

Very often, of course, mental illness can be so complex, and professional help so limited, that chemical and mechanical remedies are the only realistic, available treatments. Also, there are some disturbed persons who will need supportive help most of their lives, just as a chronic diabetic or heart patient may need lifetime medical attention. However, in terms of what we know about the nature of mental illness, we should be slow to replace the "talking out" process with a *purely* medicinal remedy, especially in *neurotic* cases.

Finally, clergymen, too, have been reluctant to give full acceptance to psychiatry. While the philosopher says, "We shall help this man think straight and he will be well," or the lawyer says, "We shall punish him and he will be well," or the doctor says, "We shall give him a bottle of pills and he will be well," the clergyman may say, "The difficulty with this man is that he does not pray enough, or go to the sacraments, or he does not want to use the spiritual aids that we have for him; and if he would only listen to us, he would be well."

The philosopher, the physician, the judge, the warden and the clergyman have all believed they hold the key to mental health and that it is their primary prerogative to foster it. But we must remind ourselves that mental illness is essentially an emotional thing, rooted in feeling, with its origins at work in early childhood when the young child is a feeling person, not a thinking person.

The child's unconscious is like an undeveloped X-ray plate on which every experience, every fright, every relationship is recorded, indelibly registered. In later years one may not remember the events of childhood. Usually we do not remember the most painful things. That is why psychoanalysis is so interesting and so difficult. It brings back into the patient's consciousness the things that were most painful and most significant in his early development, things which are buried, hidden, but which are there, nevertheless, influencing his feelings and his adult experiences.

This is a simple, maybe too simple, explanation of the unconscious, that vast treasure house of hidden experiences and especially of hidden feelings which we carry with us. A person's mental health depends on what kind of marks his early emotional experiences left upon his unconscious and to what extent he was able to survive the frights and worries and insecurities that every human being feels.

The unconscious is a very real dimension of the human personality. This is proven again and again in psychoanalytic treatment. Most people accept the existence of the unconscious. They see it at work in slips of the tongue which indicate the presence, in the unconscious, of material thought to have been completely forgotten. They see it at work in hypnosis. How else explain the fact that a person, having been put in a trance by a hypnotist, can recall things he has not remembered in fifty or sixty years? He can sit down and regress to three or four years of age and write his name as he wrote it at the age of three in childish block letters, thus pulling out of the hidden past the experiences that had meaning at another time and are still at work in the unconscious!

A question that usually occurs to those who reflect on these matters for the first time is: what happens to free will? What happens to merit, to sanctity and to all the things that are important to us in our Christian theology and philosophy regarding freedom of choice?

To begin with, we can see psychology as the handmaid of theology and the spiritual life. Psychology can and does give us insights that not only help us live holier, less sinful lives, but also healthier and happier lives. Let me illustrate. Everyone has some particular fault, some failing in conduct into which it seems easy to fall. Some people get along well with their parents; others do not. Some people have little trouble with sexuality; others are constantly plagued by it. Some have no trouble with authority; others find it most difficult to accept. Some break one of the Ten Commandments; others break another. Psychology helps us understand these variants by giving us insight into why we act differently in certain instances, showing us the part that past emotional experiences play in our lives.

We all have problems with our emotions. There are a few very happy, well-adjusted, holy people; a few very sick people. The rest are somewhere in between. A newly ordained priest need hear confessions for only a month or two before he becomes aware that many of the problems presented to him in the confessional could be alleviated with the help of psychological insight as well as spiritual counsel.

We may very well ask: what happens to free will and sanctity in view of the tremendous emotional forces working in the unconscious which influence at least some of our actions? Freud, the discoverer of the unconscious, was accused of denying the existence of free will. In reality, he, probably more than any other man of our time, has been responsible for liberating the will. He has helped us to see and to understand how feelings and emotions can get in the way of the will making free, untrammeled choices. He has taught us to discover, through psychoanalytic insight, why we are subject to compulsive thoughts and actions, why we are sometimes trapped in antisocial or immoral patterns.

In understanding why man acts as he does and in discovering the original painful experiences that lie at the root of some of his antisocial or immoral actions, we find that the will can be loosed from the influences which hindered it, which made its functioning and free choice difficult. With insight comes control and with control comes freedom. That is why one good Catholic psychoanalyst could say that the person who has been analyzed well is equally capable of great good *or* great evil because, understanding so much better the things that he does, he is much more responsible for them.

Every human being is born with the faculty of free will. Whether he exercises his will or not, or the extent to which he exercises it, depends to a considerable extent on the kinds of early emotional experiences he has had.

An acute psychotic or mental defective may never exercise this faculty of free will which God made a part of his human nature. Others activate free will in varying degrees or are blocked in certain areas. When we examine as honestly as we can some of our own particular faults we see how much more difficult it is to enforce control in some areas than in others. The reason for this is that in some moral areas we may well have an emotional problem which interferes with our will's freedom. And so, to a greater or lesser extent the will is *wholly* free in very few human beings.

This situation presents a challenge to the moral theologian and the psychologist who must together reconcile the extent of freedom with the psychological conflicts and disturbances which can throttle the will and interfere with its powers of choice. This reconciliation is actually taking place. Today the theologian and the psychologist are helping each to understand the other. We have a number of priest psychologists and analysts, for example, who have no difficulty in coordinating theological and the psychological teaching concerning this effect of emotional conflict on the freedom of the will.

We are still debating the relationship between sanctity and mental health. As most psychologists see it, there is no particular problem about the achievement of sanctity by a neurotic person or even by a psychotic person. In fact, it may very well be that a person could achieve sanctity through the cross of neurosis with which God has permitted him to live. This is admittedly rather tenuous; psychologists are just beginning to explore this area, asking many questions to which we do not have the answers.

Psychologists are especially interested in the lives of certain saints who appear to have had some neurotic symptoms. The Little Flower, St. Thérèse of Lisieux, is thought by some to have achieved sanctity, at least in part, through her neurosis. There are some interesting factors in her life which would substantiate this speculation: her relationship to her father, who suffered a severe mental collapse; the fact that at a very early age she left the society she knew and entered a religious community where her sisters were in charge. These and other factors make for intriguing psychodynamic speculation. There is nothing conclusive, to be sure; admittedly, there is wide room for debate.

It must be acknowledged here that the line between the saint and the psychotic is sometimes a fine one for the casual observer to draw. Both sanctity and sickness may encourage behavior which could at times be labeled severe, depriving, self-punishing. Yet the reasons behind such actions differ mightily; the saint and the psychotic are worlds apart. The saint, who understands the full implications of his role as a member of the Mystical Body, sees the mortifications, penances and self-denials he takes upon himself as salutary ways of winning grace, strength and merit for himself and other weaker members in Christ who are in need. He achieves a kind of gratification in the knowledge that his deprivations are reaping spiritual blessings, hope and consolations for others.

The emotionally disturbed person, on the other

hand, chooses similar kinds of self-inflicted suffering, not for supernatural values, but out of his neurotic, narcissistic needs. The masochist seeks pain for its own sake, and enjoys his misery.

One of the most spectacular evidences of quite differently motivated personalities is the stigmata, the appearance of Christ's wounds on the bodies of living persons. Among at least three hundred and twenty recorded cases, only forty-one were men. There are very good reasons for believing that some of these stigmatics were very holy people (e.g., Francis of Assisi). There is also evidence to suggest that others suffered from psychosomatic symptoms of hysteria. Further collaboration between spiritual director and psychiatrist will make it easier to tell one from the other.

In any case, the possibility that certain saints were afflicted with psychic disabilities, as well as with physical suffering, should not surprise us. In fact, such a speculation should be downright consoling to many who in this tense and restless "age of anxiety" feel themselves burdened with certain neurotic-tinged emotions. If some of the saints have triumphed over mental anguish, men today can hope to achieve their eternal destiny in the face of similar afflictions.

All of these things relate, of course, to the question: how will God judge us? It seems likely that God is going to award merit to us, determine our love for Him, and assign us our place in heaven, in terms, not of an objective standard but rather of the degree of rational control that we are able to bring to our living of the spiritual life. If the psychotic only makes one or two valid and free judgments in his life, he will be judged by these, and he may be canonized in God's eyes. Perhaps the people who seemingly lead such blameless and spotless lives may be far down the list as God reckons things because they have been endowed with an emotional stability which could have achieved far greater virtue with comparative ease. (This is an oversimplified explanation of an area which needs a great deal more thought and study.)

In view of all this, one can see why psychologists are so concerned about the importance of training the child. An important recent book is *Love or Constraint* by Father Marc Oraison, M.D., published by The Paulist Press. This is a little treatise on the emotional implications of the religious training of the young child. It is a theoretical discussion of what ingredients should go into the development of the child in his early years so that he will grow up to be a healthy, positive, receptive kind of person instead of a fearful, timorous and insecure one. The religious area is just one aspect of a much broader relationship between children, parents and the enveloping world.

Two important aspects of growing maturity are emotional attitudes towards authority and sexuality. We must give careful attention to the way in which these develop in the personality, in the psychological nooks and crannies of the child's life. It is good for a child to be permitted to grow in an open, hopeful, venturesome kind of way, not overly fearful lest a mistake or two put him outside the pale. A child should feel free to make mistakes because this is one way men learn.

Even as adults, some occasionally profit from their mistakes.

To learn to have a wholesome attitude toward authority during childhood is of primary importance for a person's mental health. Children must be taught how to accept the necessary direction and leadership of someone who has the right to exercise it, whether a parent, the Church, the clergy or God Himself. Children should learn to look confidently toward authority rather than to regard it with resentment or fear. The problem of authority, even more than sexuality, is perhaps the most serious problem today.

However, another ingredient necessary to mental health is the child's acceptance of his sexuality. The lack of proper sex education in the early years of childhood is still a serious defect not only in Catholic circles but in American families generally. Sex is still a puzzle to many young people. The development in children of the right *attitude* toward sex—more important even than information about it—often comes too late. Children should grow up learning about sexuality as naturally as they learn about any other of the innumerable subjects in which children are interested. Not only should they receive answers, but they should feel comfortable in discussing sexuality. Sexuality is a part of life, and a growing awareness of its reality and importance should be encouraged. Unless this happens early, unless sex can be freely talked about in the home, casually and respectfully, sexual problems of some kind or other are likely to develop later.

A third ingredient important to mental health is a

sound preparation for marriage. In failing to provide a *practical* education for marriage our Catholic schools are often just as much behind the times as any others. Our young people are often not ready for marriage. Some Catholic school systems are changing that situation. In the Archdiocese of New York, for example, Monsignor George A. Kelly has written a number of easy-to-read books on the subject; there is a flourishing pre-Cana movement; and a course in preparation for marriage is compulsory for every high school senior class. However, much of this comes too late. Many of the teachers in our schools need a course in marriage and family life themselves, so that even an elementary grade teacher can speak meaningfully and in detail of a vocation which 90 per cent of his or her students will embark on.

Our shortcomings are obvious in terms of the many Catholic marriages which encounter trouble. Jesuit sociologist Father John Thomas has pointed out that in many ways the Catholic family is not very different from any other American family. Often the members of the American Catholic family, despite many years of Catholic influence, are no happier or holier than their non-Catholic neighbors.

We must learn to talk about marriage in our schools and to parents in real life terms. It seems that we are not doing this yet. We are making some exciting inroads into this field, but we need more research, and much more practice-teaching to find the best formula for educating children for marriage.

Finally, a word or two about counselling and psychotherapy. One need have no worry about a Catholic who goes to a good professional. For the good psychotherapist will respect the philosophical, ethical and religious convictions of his patient and will not tamper with them in any way. In the great majority of cases the good psychotherapist can solve a patient's emotional difficulties within the framework of his faith, Jewish, Protestant or Catholic. It is the incompetent psychiatrist who invades the value system of his patient, telling him what to do or what not to do. That is not good technique.

Sometimes, as a preliminary to treatment, it is necessary for the psychiatrist to help his client face the genuineness of his convictions. Are they really deep? Does he really understand his faith? If there seems to be some confusion as to what the patient's religion teaches or does not teach, the competent psychiatrist will suggest that the patient talk this over with the priest or rabbi or minister.

If something comes up in the treatment of a patient that is absolutely not in the psychiatrist's sphere of competence or that touches the area of the emotions and passions in such a way that they cannot be dealt with apart from the patient's religious convictions, the psychiatrist will usually seek collaboration with an understanding clergyman to whom he may send his patient.

We have tried to give a brief sketch of some of the things important to the interrelationship of our Faith with another great science, psychology, acknowledged by modern popes and theologians as immensely helpful in bringing solace to the suffering soul.

The Church has always used every device within

her reach to improve the present life and future destiny of her children. She has called upon music, art, philosophy, literature and ritual; she has borrowed from all things that are important to man. Now she is happy to acknowledge a new handmaiden, the healing science of psychiatry.

Psychology and Married Love

REV. ROBERT W. GLEASON, S.J.*

MODERN PSYCHOLOGY has made a great number of contributions to the understanding of love and especially of married love. Along with the exploration of techniques of sexual adjustment there have been many studies of the nature of human love in general and many descriptive analyses of the growth of married love through its various stages of youth, middle age, and old age. J. Guitton's delightful little book on *Human Love* gives a detailed picture of the genesis and development of love through all its phases and some very wise counsel on ways to preserve love intact.

It has often been remarked how difficult it is to speak at all of love because of the semantic problem.

* Chairman of the Department of Theology at Fordham University, Father Robert Gleason, S.J., is one of America's theologians widely read in Europe, with more than a score of editions in French, German, Italian, Spanish, Dutch and Portuguese. Of his five books, four have been best sellers in the United States. Father Gleason's articles have appeared in many theological journals in this country and abroad.

The term itself is used in widely different senses and there are highly diverse types of love: parental, marital, filial, fraternal, and love of friendship, to mention but a few. Then, of course, authorities differ considerably on what we might call the philosophy of love, its essence and meaning. In this essay we make no pretensions to offer something new on the subject or even to construct a new synthesis of the views of other writers. And, of course, nothing like completeness can be hoped for in a few pages. Instead, what we have done is to outline a few points which we hope will prove a help to the reader in grasping the complexity of the subject and in encouraging further study. In addition, the selection is arbitrary; many others could have been chosen for discussion and perhaps should have been.

Even the very number of the theories on love may seem startling to the average man, who feels that common sense and experience could settle some of the questions discussed. But philosophers and writers have had many different opinions in the course of history on this interesting subject.

Some of the earlier students of love were interested in cosmological love rather than love in its plenary, personal meaning. To Plato love was a sort of inverse gravity, drawing the soul away from the world of sense to the eternal and valid world of the Forms. To Aristotle love was a metaphysical appetite inherent in all reality, summoning it to its proper perfection and development. In the creationist framework of Christianity, however, this cosmic love truly justifies its name, for Christianity sees God as producing the world by a gesture of creative love and by the same gesture directing all creation back to Him through a dynamism implicit in its very nature, a natural dynamism that we may call the creature's natural love of God. Although Bonaventure prefers to discuss love in terms of persons rather than of cosmic forces, declaring that love represents simply the union of the concupiscible faculty with its object, nevertheless in his description of alterocentric love the saint goes beyond this somewhat bare definition to suggest that love is an *acumen penetrans,* a revelation of the proper individuality of the person loved. His emphasis is on the concrete persons given in love and loved, not, however, as an assemblage of qualities, but as individuals.[1]

Bonaventure had recognized two fundamentally different types of love, self-love and altruistic love; succeeding generations of scholasticism set themselves the task of reconciling and reducing this duality to unity, if it were at all possible. Unlike some writers who seem to feel that authentic Christianity destroyed self-love in order to ensure the development of selfless love, Christian thinkers generally did not attempt so drastic and facile a solution to this complicated problem. All admitted that love could not be entirely without regard for self since man was a bundle of needs with legitimate demands for his self-development.

St. Thomas lent to the problem a wise and moderate humanist's attention, and more than one sketch of a solution is to be found in his works. Some of his commentators suggested that the self that knows itself as a

[1] R. Prentice, *The Psychology of Love according to St. Bonaventure* (New York: The Franciscan Institute, 1951), ch. 3.

part of a higher whole will naturally love the good of the whole more than its private good. Others declared that the final solution of St. Thomas to the meaning of love is to be found in his image analogy. Man loves himself as an image and in loving himself properly as an image naturally has greater love for that of which he is the image. Whether this solution is complete or not is still under discussion. The English Jesuit M. D'Arcy pointed out that one may love an image in either of two ways: perfecting the image by casting off all care except for the original or loving the original by developing the virtualities of the image.[2]

Modern scholars seem less preoccupied with finding and justifying a definition of love than with providing the reader a vicarious experience of the reality itself. They stress the interiority, the subjectivity of love, and when they do offer a definition it is only in passing, leaving it to us to decide from the accompanying descriptive phenomena whether it be true or not.

According to some the meaning of human love is the deliverance of individuality through the sacrifice of egoism. Love urges us to acknowledge in another the unconditional central significance of which, in virtue of our egoism, we are conscious in our own selves. Through faith we affirm the importance and dignity of the loved person as he or she exists in God and possesses everlasting significance. The object of love is thus twofold: in the first place we love the ideal beloved, who belongs to another and higher sphere of being and whom we install

[2] M. C. D'Arcy, *The Mind and Heart of Love* (New York: Henry Holt and Company, 1947), ch. 3.

in our ideal world. In the second place we love the natural human creature, who furnishes the living, personal material for the realization of the ideal, not through subjective imagination but through objective transformation or regeneration.

Much of what modern thinkers say about love recalls the analyses of Max Scheler. Scheler has defined love as a movement passing from a lower value to a higher one in which the higher value of the person flashes upon us. "Love is that movement wherein every concrete individual object possessing worth achieves the highest value compatible with its nature and vocation; or wherein it attains the ideal state of value intrinsic to its nature."[3]

Scheler rejects as too static the view that love is merely a contemplation of values already realized; yet he also objects to those who see love as a promotion of values. This, he feels, would be "educative" and therefore opposed to love since it is not in the nature of love as such to desire a change in the thing loved. Scheler seems to think that love creates higher values in the beloved by the mere fact of its existence, and that all change is opposed to the ideal image of the beloved, which to him is so important. But change can be development and one does not change the beloved essentially in causing him or her to develop to perfection, to realize all the good that is implicit and latent. His statement: "Love and the pedagogic attitude cannot coexist as simultaneous phenomena" seems exaggerated, for it

[3] M. Scheler, *The Nature and Forms of Sympathy* (New Haven: Yale University Press, 1954), p. 160.

ignores the fact that the very object of our love is a being in time, subject to process, involving an invitation to maturity, possessing a dynamism to fulfill the virtualities of its own ideal paradigm. On Scheler's supposition it would seem impossible to love a child and simultaneously to hope that it will grow to maturity. Moreover he seems to feel that this mysterious movement of love is a passing from real values to equally real values, but these later values have as yet only an ideal existence in the eye of the lover.

In love, Scheler claims, there is no attempting to fix an objective, no deliberate shaping of purpose aimed at the higher value and its realization; love itself in the course of its own movement is what brings about the continuous emergence of ever-higher value in the object—just as if it were streaming out of the object of its own accord, without any sort of exertion (even of wishing) on the part of the lover. Scheler is apparently saying that the lover tries not to alter the fundamental divine idea and pattern of the beloved but to cooperate with it by permitting it an erosphere in which it may naturally evolve and grow in accordance with its own individual rhythm. But the lover need not maintain a purely passive attitude towards values in the beloved.

Scheler's great contribution to the theory of love, however, was his insistence on the knowledge that accompanies it—that somehow the concrete individuality of the other in all its "thisness" is given as a unit. His own analysis of love, excluding as it does all intention to give, falls into the error he himself deprecated, that of fixing the gaze upon real and ideal values. Yet it is to his credit that he has contributed an excellent phenomenological refutation of the theory that all love is a mere disguise for the activity of the sexual instinct.

M. Nedoncelle opens his analysis by a definition of love as a will for the promotion of the values of the beloved. The loving subject wills above all else the autonomous existence and development of a "Thou" according to the immanent trends of the values the "I" has discovered therein. The primordial élan of love is not only a movement of the soul toward the other and his intimate values but it is also an energy bent on the realization of something: it wishes to contribute to the existence and fulfillment of the other according to the unique vocation of the other. Love is then a pathetic intervention, a vigorous engagement, in tension toward the fulfillment of the "Thou." Does this mean that love is a will to re-create the beloved? It means, at least, that the human lover strives to affirm the existence of the other and to contribute to his development. Love begins with the perception of values but love does not rest there in a lazy contemplation; it intervenes to ratify and accept, to promote. Every lover is convinced in love that he is able to influence another's consciousness and to produce, in a certain sense, a growth of an autonomous interiority.[4]

Nedoncelle insists upon two other fundamental characteristics of the phenomenon of love: a desire to be loved and an implication that one is already loved. He disagrees with the Protestant scholar Nygren's pre-

[4] M. Nedoncelle, *Vers une Philosophie de l'Amour* (Paris: Aubier, 1946), pp. 19–25.

tended antinomy between the two loves, reminding us that it is only the limits, the deficiencies of Eros, that are condemnable, not Eros herself, and that Eros herself condemns these limits because Eros discovers that her vocation is to liberality.

According to Nedoncelle, the very fact that one loves involves a minimum of reciprocity. If I truly love another he has already enriched me by his sole presence open to my perception, and my love must begin with thanksgiving that he is. He, the other, has not decided perhaps to give himself to me in particular, but by willing to be himself and to deploy his activity in the world he has made himself transparent to me; every personal existence, by its existence in the world, is a minimum of personal goodness offered to the public, an initial movement of self-revelation which is an invitation, implicit and general, to love.

But love wishes for more than this: it wishes for the maximum of reciprocity. This reciprocity Nedoncelle discovers in four successive degrees. At the lowest point the other responds to my will to promotion by the sheer fact of existing; witness the child or the sick man who is loved. In the next step the reciprocity has become psychological: the other perceives my project, even if he rejects it or ignores its author. But my intention has reached him. It has attached itself to his substance, as, according to Newman, the early Christians attached themselves to their persecutors. A third level is reached when the subject ratifies my plans for him. Thus the teacher is delighted if the student accepts his insights.

Finally the circle is complete when the other turns toward me the same loving will to promotion that I have turned to him.

Thus the whole four stages are willed by anyone who loves; wishing that the other be loving, that he be a value, I wish him to love that in me by which I can love him and will to love him; that is, I wish him to love. Love is an invocation: "I count on something in you to render me capable of loving you; I wish, it is true, that you be generous enough in certain cases to forget me (for the sake of others) but even there you will be recompensing me."

Perhaps the most interesting part of Nedoncelle's analysis is his discussion of the spiritual community that love creates. Love, he says, creates a We; an I-for-Thou community. Each rejoices to foster a richness that he does not possess in himself. Each has a sort of having in the other, a centrifugal possession. In a certain sense each exists in the other; the "we" is the crossing of these two "havings in the other." The consciousness of this double generous transposition is the meaning of love. This communion of subjects implies a coexistence of two decentered series, where the individual qualities can freely circulate in the continuity of persons. There results a certain heterogeneous identity of "I" and "Thou," for the "I" wishes that the "Thou" be and is at the same time wished by the "Thou." By this mutual desire for promotion the two come as close as possible to sharing an identity.

This "We" is dynamic, for it constantly foreshadows a still higher unity. Each degree of union that it evokes in us awakens the fear of disunion and carries us on in the search for a closer union.

This fundamental, personal type of I-for Thou union, with this reciprocity of consciousness, seems to be restricted in its depth to a dyad. Hence to Nedoncelle love will be a conscious, reciprocal, generous "having" in the other, a reciprocity of consciousness based on a self-giving, a mutual desire for promotion of values.

For Guitton, less preoccupied to define than most authors, the essence of love is a self-donation. "The psychological mechanism by which love begins might be called a double illusion for it is at once the projection of an ideal on the beloved and the reception of an ideal image of oneself. This is quite different from the self-donation which is the essence of love."[5]

All of these analyses seem to us to have certain notes in common; all stress that love is self-donation; that it is also self-realization inasmuch as it is a good that befalls man; that it results in an intimate union of consciousness between the two persons who love, that it implies two limitless desires: the intention to give everything possible to the beloved and the intention to unite with the beloved in the highest possible degree.[6] Even in wounded love both of these intentions are infinite in their immanent trends. Finally, most authors stress that the genesis of love is somehow based upon an

[5] J. Guitton, *Essay on Human Love* (New York: Philosophical Library, 1951), ch. 4.

[6] D. von Hildebrand, *Marriage* (New York: Longmans Green and Company, 1942), pp. 28–35.

intuition of the values, realized and virtual, of the person loved.

It seems to us that the course of the development in time of human love reveals its nature as a total response of the spirit poised in an unstable equilibrium of three elements, the carnal, the effective, and the free. In each is a tendency to develop independently of the others.[7]

The carnal aspect, which is opaque, instinctive, has as its function to incarnate love, to reify it, to give it a definitive and extramental reality. In so giving it body it causes the whole person to awaken from the heavy slumber of passive matter and to vibrate with life, wholly informed as it is by the new sentiment. Unfortunately, as instinct, it constantly tends to disassociate itself from the good of the whole since it is not selective, exclusive, or donative. If, however, it is controlled and kept within the synthesis, it then incorporates love and serves in a unique fashion as an instrument of revelation and of knowledge.

The affective element, which lends a new vigor even to sense-perception, openly brings to light secret intimations of infinity in love. It is the dimension most dwelt on in experience, which provides the stimulus to generosity, the basis for faith in love, and that religious atmosphere of love, the erosphere, which offers to intelligence and to intuition the possibility of discovering what is already implied in this experience: the existence of a higher, personal unity which alone can bring about

[7] J. Mouroux, *The Meaning of Man* (New York: Sheed and Ward, 1948), ch. 9.

the immanent trends of love—infinite donation and infinite union. The affective dimension affords love its plenitude, impulse, energy; it alone redeems sexuality by lending it intelligibility and by fostering an absolutely exclusive and eternal union of the most profound tenderness and spirituality which is experienced as having the character of a gift. Lending to the body as well as to the soul the "wings" of which Plato spoke it assumes and spiritualizes the body, for it is itself an epiphany of both body and soul.

This second element of affectivity also has a tendency to succumb to the temptations of Narcissus, to believe that its own intoxication can be stimulated apart from the special function of confining carnality to that exclusivity demanded by nature. It is tempted to liberate itself from its finality, to invite body and will to many loves, and is then startled and bewildered to find its essence corrupted and disintegrating, itself acting out a mere parody of the vital love it had formerly experienced.

The third element in the synthesis is that of free decision, which is able to ratify by its creative and irrevocable *fiat* the affective impulses in a union which is permanent. This is the element that makes personal the suggestions of nature as it freely follows the *logos* of love. Yet the will is always tempted to substitute for the nature of love a nature of its own creation that would involve less giving of the self. Disappointed when it sees that the creative consent did not fix immutably the love situation, thus rendering love immune to all possibility of disappointment, the will can also be tempted to substitute a less arduous relationship, perhaps one of friendship. It is tempted to consider the aspirations of affectivity as mere illusion when it finds that it is not at all the master of time and has not achieved, through its decision, perfect love at once. And finally, when it realizes that the stages through which love must pass in order to grow cannot be abbreviated, it is very much tempted to shrink from its task of ensuring that in the marital union the soul be as active as the body. Should it yield to this temptation there begins a disassociation of the three elements of love which may well lead to love's disintegration.

As Hildebrand points out, the personal mystery sealed in the body of the partner, the spouse, can be ignored in the very act destined to operate the revelation of that secret, and the will, whose function it is to guide the increasing penetration in knowledge, can remain content with the assumption that the partner has no longer anything to say. In a word, the will can bring about the finitization of love. For, the will, whose task it is to accept the sacrifices that make possible a We-communion as well as an I-Thou communion, can refuse to do so; declining responsibility for time and duration, it can seek the infinite in a moment and value only the moment. Instead of introducing the eternal into duration through time, it can attempt a vain immobilization of the infinite in a timeless now.

Love needs constant care at each of its stages if it is to survive. The moment we fail to see the beloved partner from within, the moment we see him or her from without, as other people would see him or her, we lessen our first vision of the deeper meaning of the beloved's character and are already somewhat unfaithful to our love. Love is a task as well as a gift. For those who see love as deceit, infatuation, a trick of nature to ensure continuity to the race, it is only natural that love should fade, wither, and die. But for the Christian who sees love and marriage as a reflection of the union of God with the soul, of Christ with His Church, of the *Verbum* with His manhood, love is a gift to be preserved. Hence married partners must strive to perfect their original self-gift through all the sacrifices that time demands. They must try to preserve a sense of gratitude to God for the great gift of love, to preserve a sense of the mysterious truth that another person's love has been entrusted to them. They must avoid all that would militate against love; in particular the permanent fixing of love at any one of the stages of its growth. They must avoid, to use a Freudian term in a translated sense, "arrested development" in love, and act to meet the three great summons of the love to growth: the difficult initial stages of marriage, the shattering disillusion of middle age, and the final death of passion in old age.

If love is to meet all the challenges well, it should develop from the more sensual to the more spiritual, it should widen to include the community and it should fulfill its inner trend to become supernaturalized in Christ and become progressively more and more a manifestation of unselfish Christian charity.

The High Cost of Discrimination

Rev. Philip S. Hurley, S.J.*

Prejudice has been studied from the social point of view and from the point of view of psychology. It has not received so much attention from the moral point of view. Yet in this area more lasting harm to our nation can be done because a weakening of the moral fibre of the people can have particularly deteriorating effects.

Social and psychological studies show the harm done to the person discriminated against. Analysis of the moral consequences reveals the harm done to the one discriminating. The conscience of one who discriminates is warped in more than one direction. When man cultivates a false moral estimate in one area, he tends to debase his moral judgments in others. Fostering ideas which arise from emotional dislike brings about a

* Ordained in 1939, Father Hurley has taught theology to college men at Georgetown and Fordham for the past seventeen years. Since 1955 he has been assistant chaplain of the Catholic Interracial Council of New York. He has added to his work in this field the function of assistant editor of the monthly magazine, *Interracial Review*.

general lowering of the total moral tone. There is an unacknowledged hypocrisy constantly at work, vitiating one's judgments in other lines. Inevitably this indulgence affects other value-judgments. In time of crisis it will tend to belie the outward proclamation of ideals and still seek justification for its ways.

If we multiply this process across the entire nation, allow it to work in the minds of millions of people, we will have an erosion of moral standards that can wreck the ideals of a nation. Gordon Allport, in his well-known study, *The Nature of Prejudice* (Doubleday, 1958), estimates that "four-fifths of the American population harbors enough antagonism toward minority groups to influence their daily conduct." The only saving feature he sees in the situation is that the "cross-currents of hostility somehow neutralize one another; and an ultimate obedience to the democratic creed serves as a further restraint."

Outward discrimination in its turn tends to fortify existing prejudice. It seeks justification for its presence. It lends the support of accepted practice to the perpetuation of social institutions. When years go by without any challenge forthcoming, discriminatory practice becomes installed almost by prescription. Only a major eruption can then dislodge it. The prejudices that nourish and sustain discrimination continue as routine, accepted and normal modes of thought.

Hence prejudice is socially dangerous. Contrary to popular opinion it is not something that begins and ends with the individual but has repercussions throughout society. Failure to recognize the menace that is prejudice accounts for the fact that many well-meaning citizens can be the more or less unwitting transmitters of the disease of racial discrimination.

Most people recognize the evils of discrimination. They fail to realize that discrimination is the fruit of prejudice and that they themselves are often responsible for keeping alive those attitudes which result in discrimination. A tragic irony is hidden here, too, because prejudiced people are the sad agents of their own destruction. What should be subjected to careful study is the way in which one can be trapped into indulging in those attitudes over which he does have control, concerning which he should make careful examination of conscience. We can no longer attribute these harmful attitudes to upbringing or environment and consider ourselves thereby excused.

Prejudice can, of course, be quite innocuous. Generally we classify harmless prejudices as "taste" or "inclination" to one style or form of attachment over another. We often entertain prejudices that are harmless in this sense. Familiar instances can be seen in the support of favorite sports teams, in selecting our clothes, in interior decorating, in a hundred forms of self-structured attitudes that do no one any harm whatsoever. In everyday speech the word "prejudice," however, is usually reserved for those attitudes that involve one's estimate of the neighbor. If that estimate is unfair to him, founded on insufficient evidence, one is guilty of injustice.

Hence when prejudice begins to affect attitudes toward the neighbor, one has to exert some checks. Here we enter the field of morals that falls under the Eighth

Commandment of the Decalogue. That commandment forbids us to bear false witness against our neighbor. The precise fault in this case is given by moralists the title of "rash judgment."

One may go through life entertaining a number of false conclusions; for centuries men went along with the conviction that the world was flat. But that kind of error does no harm to another human being. Prejudice is the form of rash judgment that does harm to the reputation of another. Rash judgment is sustained on a false premise. If we have reason to suspect the truth of our premises, we are obliged to check them lest we be guilty of cultivating erroneous conclusions. We are obliged, then, to find out what makes a judgment "rash," why it does not conform to objective truth. If we neglect to do so, we may be contributing to an estimate that does harm to our neighbor.

When one finds that he is indulging in an erroneous estimate of another, yet passes that judgment along, he is then guilty of lowering someone else's esteem. An injustice has been done to the first individual. He has a right to his reputation, to a just estimate of his worth on the part of others and no one may interfere with that evaluation. The third party may, up to this point, have had a fair opinion of the individual; perhaps he was indifferent to his status. If by my action the first person has been deprived of the reputation he deserves, I have been guilty of an infringement of his God-given dignity. For this the individual is answerable in terms of the virtue of charity which demands that one manifest to all men the respect to which their innate dignity as children of God entitles them. When my judgment of another is such as to lessen my own regard for his reputation, I am likewise guilty of injustice.

But suppose no one knows I have such an attitude? What then? Surely I do no one any harm if that prejudiced attitude remains within the sanctuary of my own mind. We have often met this argument in the area of immoral literature and immoral entertainment. We have learned that simply because the bad thoughts produced by pornographic literature remain within the mind of the reader, they are not the less harmful. Because a person watches a lewd performance on the stage is no reason to think that harmful thoughts have not been roused that can eventually cause the subject personal damage and society moral deterioration.

Every man, we are taught by Christian morality, has a right to the esteem of his fellow men unless he has forfeited it by personal actions or behavior. If rash suspicions or opinions about others merely lessen but do not destroy an individual's reputation, the suspicion or opinion is usually not more than a venial sin. But defective thinking can at times be gravely sinful because from these thoughts there flow, as an effect from a cause, defaming speech and damaging actions. Oftentimes, as men think, so they speak, and as they speak, so they act.

When an entire group is the object of such rash judgments and such defaming speech, the consequences are all the greater.

When rash judgment as we have described it is externalized in the form of actions that dishonor another in his presence, it is called contumely. Contumely sins against justice and charity because it goes against a person's right to honor and the external marks of respect that accord with his character and standing.

Where eighteen million of our fellow Americans are the constant object of defaming speech and damaging actions, we ought to be appalled at the harm that is continuously being done to them. Where private thoughts serve to perpetuate those false attitudes and rash judgments, the area of infection widens.

Prejudice is an experience that is common to all men; it is really a by-product of original sin. We all recognize the impulses within us that incline us to indulge in prejudice just as we see within our nature other impulses that have to be controlled and mastered if we are to lead Christian lives. It should come as no surprise to discover that we have prejudices; the fault would be to neglect to uproot them. Background, environment, upbringing all contribute to the judgments that motivate much of our conduct. But mature life has taught us how to adjust many of our childhood estimates. Why do we cling to childish attitudes towards those of other races?

The answer to that is likely to be found in our unwillingness to discard opinions to which we have become attached, attitudes around which we have built certain favorite concepts, those which tend to flatter our ego or serve to sustain preconceived ideas of our own importance. There must always be some other individual who is lower on the social scale than we are. The extraordinary social mobility in American life somehow does not leave us with a desire to see others escape the errors we made, the handicaps we faced.

For this reason prejudice enshrines the social taboos that render the American dream of equal opportunity impossible of fulfillment. Danger to public opinion, to the proper consensus of judgment, has been initiated. The entire nation is bound to suffer. Allport acknowledges that Gunnar Myrdal has touched this sore spot in his classic study, *The American Dilemma*:

To him [Myrdal] the crux of the whole issue is the inner "moral uneasiness" white Americans suffer at failing to make their practice conform to the American creed. The dilemma is: "the ever-raging conflict between, on the one hand, the valuations preserved on the general plane which we shall call the 'American creed,' where the American thinks, talks and acts under the influence of high national and Christian precepts, and, on the other hand, the valuations on specific planes of individual and group living, where personal and local interests; economic, social and sexual jealousies; consideration of community prestige and conformity; group prejudice against particular persons or types of people; and all sorts of miscellaneous wants, impulses, and habits dominate his outlook."
The average American, therefore, experiences moral uneasiness and a feeling of individual and collective guilt. He lives in a state of conflict (p. 313).

Such is the damage done within the individual and collective conscience; let us examine also the way in which social institutions support prejudice and solidify discrimination. Social scientists have enumerated a number of such "arrangements"; we shall examine a few. Failure to perceive that discrimination gathers strength from our entire system of social relations is what makes many of us dupes of the social system under which we live. We have grown used to them, we take them for granted, we have never challenged their right to exist; the result is that we have been supporting certain processes that we would repudiate were someone to unmask their basic injustice.

In the United States white people make many generalizations about the Negro. With scarcely any reflection, many of them have judged that the Negro is by nature of lower intelligence, lazy, inefficient, given to petty thievery and lacking in sexual control. What gives generalizations like these a recognized and accepted position is that they have never been tested. The weight of the past holds them in our store of favored judgments. We never take the trouble to check their validity. Because many Americans preserve such judgments unchallenged for a long time, they are reluctant to see them dislodged.

It is because of attitudes such as these that the axiom has become true of the Negro, "last to be hired, first to be fired." Habitual practice, traditional patterns, as long as they enjoy general approval, are not readily upset.

In an illuminating study made by the New School for Social Research in 1959 for the New York State Commission Against Discrimination, entitled "Discrimination and Low Incomes," Aaron Antonovsky made a penetrating analysis of the social meaning of discrimination. With the permission of the State Commission I shall discuss a few of the "social arrangements" listed by Dr. Antonovsky as they apply to the subject of this paper.

Social behavior is very likely to be "acceptable behavior." That is to say, we tend to do what is expected of us in a given situation. In the business world certain functions fall into patterns, expected modes of behavior. All of us tend to adopt the role that is expected without perhaps examining what is more natural or suitable for us.

Given this expectation, the individual is inclined to fulfill it. Were he to behave differently, he might encounter opposition and hostility. If the expected manner is one by which discrimination is maintained, a non-discriminatory mode of behavior will rouse opposition. Rather than provoke trouble, men go along with the prevailing group attitude. Not until the climate has changed will the individual do other than what is expected of him. Because the expected behavior has the sanction of the group it also appears "right"; what "has always been done" thus becomes "the right thing to do."

Next we find "isolating mechanisms," patterns which operate to keep the victims of discrimination from access to the tools necessary to break down the barriers. Only since the Supreme Court decision of May 17, 1954, on desegregation in the schools have we become alert to the many forms by which these isolating mechanisms function. Thus, for example, it came as a surprise to many people to learn of the "gerrymandering" that has blocked Negro voting, the reprisals that serve to restrain protest, the inherent inequality of the old "separate but equal" doctrine in education.

Very often the question is asked, "What is the Negro doing to help himself?" People who ask this question frequently have no idea of the apathy that is produced by poverty. It does not occur to them that the Negro is caught in a vicious circle not of his own making. He is expected to improve his lot, but when he seeks to avail himself of the means of betterment, he finds himself blocked by a network of discriminating patterns.

The result is that the minority group is quite effectively kept from acquiring the means to challenge the inequities of the system. Such inequities are: "legal" harassment, exclusion from unions, a "gentlemen's agreement" that boasts of hiring Negroes yet closes the doors to Jewish employees, failure to base promotion on merit, the setting up of arbitrary quotas for hiring of minority groups, restricting certain minority groups to menial employment; in job classification, rates of pay, discriminatory practices in employee benefits, lay-off policy, profit-sharing plans, even in time allotted for vacation and sick leave! These and many other forms of unfair practice prevent people on lower level jobs from aspiring to plant leadership, foreman positions and the like.

Elmo Roper, the well-known opinion analyst, points out how discrimination affects the personality of the individual.

When the frustration of discrimination is experienced in a man's job, a whole and permanent part of his personality is eroded. His will and security, his full growth into a full human personality are stunted. His development as a citizen is retarded. And when this individual damage is multiplied to literally hundreds of thousands and millions of cases, the toll is a fearful one indeed.

Another form of isolation is seen in the case of the

Negro who does not live in an area where neighbors might inform him of a good job opportunity, or who is excluded from those groups at the plant who could enlighten him. This, too, lowers the level of his aspiration, distorts his grasp of values, tends to make him concentrate on a scale of achievement far lower than his potential. The result is that he is simply unable to recognize the advantages that lie around him, to seize the opportunities that exist.

Closely allied to isolating mechanisms are those sanctions which derive from law, custom or racial practice (acceptance). Business clubs, eating places, sports facilities may be so circumscribed that no member of a minority group may ever aspire to the advantages these facilities afford the dominant class. Pressure from alumni, restrictive covenants, associations of business, all exert an effective control that serves to maintain and perpetuate discrimination. Those who are advantageously placed in such surroundings often enjoy high standing and reputation in the most respected civic and religious groups of the community. The fact that they can at the same time subscribe to the discriminatory practices we have cited implies a double standard that approaches the hypocritical. Their children hear them extol the benefits, advantages and general emolument that they derive from restrictive practices. This leads young people generally to develop such judgments for themselves. As students they aspire to those standards while at the same time they proclaim their country as the land of opportunity and equality.

Even where policy formulation recognizes the rights

of minority groups, there is possible a form of evasion that amounts to outright discrimination. Where business firms, industrial plants, associations of various kinds fail to live up to their proclaimed policy of anti-discrimination, the whole intent of the law or the policy is subverted. Numerous are the devices that office or plant management can discover to impede or block the effective execution of administrative policy. Not only do those discriminated against suffer; younger members of the firm have their values distorted, their conception of equality debased, their trust in the integrity of industry destroyed.

Not infrequently, well-meaning people who genuinely wish to do something to remove discriminatory practices are held back by "anticipatory fears." Social reprisals, loss of reputation, exclusion from opportunities of promotion—these are some of the means by which an offended community can retaliate against the reformer or the nonconformist. The slow progress of integration in many communities can be explained by these fears. Only the hardiest will risk possible loss to brave the hostility of a life-long environment.

Surrounding, supporting and uniting these mechanisms of discrimination is a way of thinking, an ideology, which is invoked to justify the inferior status of the excluded group. Favorite clichés about the latter's inferiority, stereotypes that classify according to some visible characteristic are constantly brought forward to fortify the structure of the discriminating pattern. If the minority group is readily distinguishable by virtue of color, language or dress, the barriers tend to become more rigid, the ideology more intense. Whatever one perceives as setting the group apart is heightened, even distorted, in the direction of justifying discriminatory behavior. The social patterns of discrimination in turn serve to reinforce behavior. The two then go together to support one another.

Stereotypes woven into everyday life intensify the process: in literature (*Uncle Tom's Cabin*); in children's games and songs ("eenie, meenie, minie, mo . . ."); in entertainment and mass media (Aunt Jemima, minstrel shows), in the Negro domestic; and in the prejudicial conversation of parents (Antonovsky, *op. cit.*).

All these experiences confirm the growing child in his beliefs about social relationships; he accepts all as a matter of course. It would simply never occur to him that there might be a different way of viewing matters.

Sometimes his estimates admit of exceptions; but then such exceptions do not lessen the discriminatory pattern; rather they enforce it. For by noting the exception, we affirm the generalization.

Looking at the cumulative effect of these many manifestations of prejudice (and we could spend time on many more), we may begin to calculate the harm done by the more or less "innocent" cultivation of prejudice. In the study by Elmo Roper already cited, the author ventures to estimate the economic cost of discrimination.

The cost of discrimination is as great economically as it is psychologically.

If you take into account the amount of purchasing power which is denied minority groups who are paid low wages for work which could be done even more cheaply by machines, if you add the possible contribution to society by workers of minority groups who could move into high-paying vocations where there are manpower shortages—such as medicine, chemistry, engineering—if you add the costs of crime, delinquency, and social maladjustment which can be traced directly to discrimination and prejudice, and if, finally, you add the costs of segregation which are the direct result of discriminatory practices, you'll find on calculation—as I mentioned earlier—that this discrimination comes to roughly ten dollars out of every seventy-five dollar paycheck, or in total dollar terms, thirty billion dollars lost every year.

This is a pretty big market loss each year for American business. It is obvious, too, that we are some thirty billion dollars short in giving these people the economic security we constantly preach that people are entitled to under our economic system.

The economic costs are staggering; the costs to our people in terms of moral deterioration are inestimable; the loss of prestige on the international scene does incalculable damage to this country in the Cold War. These considerations may prompt us to examine carefully the high price we are paying in perpetuating discrimination.

A NOTE ON THE TYPE

IN WHICH THIS BOOK IS SET

This book is set in Fairfield, a Linotype face, created by Rudolph Ruzicka, distinguished American artist and engraver. Introduced in 1940, Fairfield is almost strictly a book type with much charm and beauty. It is easy to read as one learns from extensive reading since it furnishes some degree of stimulation and pleasure to the eye. The fitting of each letter is practically perfect, which is a real tribute to its designer. This book was composed by Progressive Typographers, Inc., of York, Pa., printed by the Wickersham Printing Company of Lancaster, Pa. and bound by Moore and Company of Baltimore, Md. The typography and design by Howard N. King.